A CASE STUDY OF
JAPANESE MIDDLE SCHOOLS
1983-1998
A Reflection on Practices,
Trends, and Issues

Nancy C. Whitman

University Press of America, ® Inc.
Lanham • New York • Oxford

ISBN 0-7618-1760-3 (cloth: alk. ppr.)
ISBN 0-7618-1761-1 (pbk: alk. ppr.)

CONTENTS

LIST OF TABLES

LIST OF FIGURES
(following page 76)

1. Location of Kitamachi Middle School, Keio Chutobu School, and Keio Futsubu School

2. School Plant and Grounds at Kitamachi Middle School

3. Sample Pages from the 8th Grade Mathematics Textbook at Kitamachi Middle School

4. Translation of Sample Pages from the 8th Grade Mathematics Textbook at Kitamachi Middle School

5. Sample Page from a Middle School Mathematics Workbook

6. Translation of Sample Page from a Middle School Mathematics Workbook

7. Sample Page from a Middle School Mathematics Drill Book

8. Translation of Sample Page from a Middle School Mathematics Drill Book

9. Sample Summary "Printo" by Kitamachi Teacher

10. Translation of Sample Summary "Printo" by Kitamachi Teacher

11. The Curriculum Building Process of Japan

ACKNOWLEDGMENT

I am forever indebted to the many individuals who made this study possible. I want to thank the administration, teachers and students of the many schools that participated in this study. I especially want to thank Mrs. Junko Gotoh, formerly of Kitamachi Middle School, Mr. Masahiro Makino of Keio Chutobu School, and Mr. Tadayuki Ishida of Keio Futsubu School.

In addition, my special thanks to Dr. Morris Lai and Dr. Irvin King who read the draft of this manuscript and made many helpful suggestions.

Translation assistance was provided by Junko Gotoh, Yoshihiko Hashimoto, Yoshihiro Hashimoto, Tadayuki Ishida, Masami Isoda, Seichi Kaida, Masahiro Makino, and Eizo Nagasaki. A special thank you for all the useful assistance.

Financial assistance for this study was partially provided by the University of Hawaii Research Council and the University of Hawaii College of Education. Funds for writing the manuscript were partially provided by the University of Hawaii Japanese Studies Endowment-funded by a grant from the Japanese Government.

FOREWORD

While several comparative studies of Japanese and United States education have been made, this one is unusual in that it spans a period of sixteen years. The schools that were studied in depth in1983 were again visited and studied in 1998. The write-ups of classroom observations are very detailed as are the programs of study. The classrooms observed were primarily middle school mathematics.

The stability of Japanese schooling is reflected when comparing Japanese schooling in 1983 and in 1998. At the same time, the schools were not stagnant as seen by the reforms taking place in Japanese education.

Although most of the classroom observations were made in middle school mathematics classrooms, the author, in her write-up, has incorporated her observations and findings regarding Japanese middle schools in general. She presents an accurate portrayal of the Japanese middle school relative to its physical appearance, student body, curriculum, basic core of studies, use of time, instruction in the classroom, and teachers.

In chapter 2, the author presents the results of studies we did jointly as part of our affiliation with the Japan-United States Teacher Education Consortium (JUSTEC). Comparisons of the geometry curriculum, student achievement, and classroom teaching between Hawaii and Japan were made.

In chapter 4, the author presents an extremely relevant discussion of those trends and issues that are of concern to educators, parents, and citizens of Japan. These items included school reform, school organization and the use of time, the curriculum, and equity issues.

In general, the author has succeeded in reaching the objectives of her study which were (1) to study the cultural basis of school practices found in the teaching of mathematics in Japanese middle schools (2) to search for explanations for the high achievements demonstrated by eighth graders on international studies (3) to describe the day-to-day teaching of middle school mathematics in sufficient detail in order to generalize and form conjectures about the teaching of mathematics in Japanese middle schools, and (4) to describe Japanese middle schools in the context of mathematics education.

For those who are interested in Japanese education, comparative education, and mathematics education, I strongly recommend the reading of this study.

Professor & Dr. Nobuhiko Nohda
Institute of Education
University of Tsukuba

PREFACE

Japan was the land of my childhood dreams to visit. Two years prior to my study of the Japanese middle (grades seven through nine) school, I visited Japan for the first time with an educational study group. That visit fulfilled my expectations of what Japan was like. However, there was so much about Japan I did not know; particularly, I did not know anything about its educational system. This was especially disconcerting since I had been an educator for more than twenty years. My wish to fill this gap prompted me to plan a serious study of Japan's educational system in the fall of 1983. At that time, Japan was in the international limelight because of its economic success and educational achievements, which added to my reasons for wanting to study the educational system. My initial interest in Japanese education led to over fifteen years of research studies with a particular focus on Japanese middle schools. This book is based on the knowledge and insights gained in these studies. The goals of this book are (1) to portray the Japanese middle school relative to its physical appearance, student body, curriculum, basic core of studies, use of time, instruction in the classroom, and teachers and (2) to identify and discuss those issues and trends that are of concern to educators, parents, and citizens in both Japan and the United States.

In general, the book is organized chronologically. The first chapter focuses on schools in Tokyo and Kyoto from 1983 until 1986. The second chapter discusses schooling in Osaka and Hokkaido in 1992 and the third chapter takes the reader in 1998 back to the school sites studied in Tokyo in 1983. The last chapter presents a discussion of the issues raised relative to middle school education in Japan and the United States, and takes a look to the future.

Nancy C. Whitman
University of Hawaii at Manoa

CHAPTER 1
INITIAL FIELD STUDY:
TOKYO, 1983-1986

Once I had decided to do research in Japan, a major task was to gain entry into the schools. This proved to be quite a formidable task and a barrier to my planned study. I soon learned how important the proper introductions were in enabling one to begin to explore possibilities of school visitations. I found out that a letter from my Dean at the University at Manoa to the Japanese Ministry of Education was of no benefit. Those people who were helpful in setting up schools as study sites and in obtaining permission to visit schools were Japanese nationals I had met when they visited the University of Hawaii, people who were former students of mine, or whom I had met through a third party via correspondence. This process of obtaining contacts and access to schools and sites took slightly more than a year. Contacts provided by private parties as compared to individuals in official capacities were utilized to obtain a typical Japanese public middle school for site study. Through these means Kitamachi Middle School became a primary focus of my field study. Since most classroom observations were made in mathematics classes (mathematics teaching being a subject I was well versed in) I, in particular, needed the support of the mathematics faculty. I also needed the support of the school administration and the board of education of the ward (district) in which the school was situated. The mathematics teacher through whom the above arrangements were made became my host teacher during my study at Kitamachi. I observed many of her classes, some of which I video taped and photographed. She not only acted as my host but she also assisted me in translating and provided information and interpretations of many activities occurring in the classroom and school.

The other major site for my field study was a private school. Arrangements for that school site were made by a former graduate student of mine. He acted as my host teacher, and I observed many of his classes. He also provided me with needed information regarding the school and translated and interpreted much of what was occurring in his classes and in those of his colleagues. In addition to note-taking, I video taped and photographed activities and classes at the schools as part of my data collecting process. Informal interviews were also used for obtaining data at both of the school sites.

To provide me with a better sense of the typicalness of the public school at which I observed, I arranged to observe seven classes, each with a different teacher in two middle schools in Kyoto After these observations, group interviews were held with the teachers observed and with the school administrators. In an attached (laboratory) school in Tokyo, four different classes, each with a different teacher, were observed, and followed-up by a group interview with the classroom teachers. In addition to the two host teachers at the major school sites, other professional friends and colleagues at the University, government, and school levels provided me with further information and interpretations of the Japanese middle school.

In summary, during the field phase of my study in the fall of 1983, a total of five middle schools were observed that included the observation of eighteen mathematics teachers. Intense observations and participation occurred at each of the site schools for approximately four weeks in the fall of 1983. Because one of my host teachers was also my house host I was able to conduct informal interviews with him very frequently. My total stay in Japan in the fall of 1983 was three months. The following April I returned to the two major sites for two weeks for further observations and interviews. And lastly, in the fall of 1986, I again visited the two school sites and interviewed the host teachers for four days.

Although this was my first experience in conducting a field study in a foreign country where the primary language is not English, this is not my first experience in conducting a field study. In fact, this is one of several studies I have conducted in the field (Whitman, 1966, 1980; Whitman & Wada, 1982). In addition, I have had numerous years of experience in classroom observations in my role as a supervisor of student teachers and as a mathematics consultant. In all of these capacities I observed approximately thirty teachers and classes over a year's time.

Study Objectives

My initial goal in conducting the field study in 1983 was to study mathematics teaching in Japanese middle schools. However, because of the marked differences between schooling in Japan and the United States, it soon became apparent that I needed to expand my goal to include studying education in general in the Japanese middle schools although the specifics are often in the mathematics area. This I did by studying documents and by conducting informal interviews in addition to the planned classroom observations. These documents and interviews focused on education in Japan's middle school as well as the teaching of mathematics. More particularly, the objectives of the study became (1) to study the cultural basis of school practices found in the teaching of mathematics in Japanese middle schools (2) to search for explanations for the high achievement in mathematics demonstrated by Japanese eighth graders in the First International Education Association mathematics tests (Husen, 1967), (3) to describe the day-to-day teaching of middle school mathematics in sufficient detail in order to generalize and form conjectures about the teaching of mathematics in Japanese middle schools, and (4) to describe Japanese middle education in the context of mathematics education. What follows is a description of how I proceeded in reaching my objectives.

Prior to entering the school sites I started to develop various checklists for classroom observation. As I became more involved with them, I began to realize the assumptions I was making about Japanese classrooms. Also I became very conscious of my own theoretical and philosophical framework. Years of training and experience in "tests and measurements" had prompted me to devise instruments to measure what might be occurring in the classes to be observed. Also influencing me was my training in the methodological tradition that regards method as "extant" prior to research. According to this orientation, scientific method involved prepared research designs and the use of analytic processes after the data were collected. Somehow this model did not seem as though it would help me answer the questions I had initially posed for the study. Also it seemed to focus my attention on details, the importance of which I had not satisfactorily established. At this point of my thinking, I abandoned any plans for coding classroom behavior via a checklist at the initial stages of observation. My intention then was to observe and take notes of as many things as possible. I was interested in doing what might yield the most meaningful information rather than being concerned whether the technique I used was "scientific." However, this is not to say that I entered the field without a frame of reference. For I did. It was based on years of experience in research and teaching school mathematics and in middle school education in general. Because it is impossible to observe and take notes on everything occurring in a classroom my framework did provide focus to my observations and note-taking. The framework with which I entered the classrooms included the following topics that had permeated much of mathematics education during the seventies and earlier and that were of concern to those in the eighties who were interested in the quality of education in American schools. At this point in time, the declining quality of American education was being brought to the attention of the public through the reports of many blue-ribbon commissions and studies including *A Nation at Risk* (NCEE, 1983).

Topics Framework

Problem-solving. The National Council of Teachers of Mathematics had recommended that problem solving be the focus of school mathematics in the 1980s (NCTM, 1980). I wondered if and how problem solving was taught in Japan's middle schools.

Time on task. First, how much time did Japanese students spend studying mathematics in school? This and questions such as the following occured to me: How is the time spaced over a years time? Over a weeks time? How is the class time utilized?

Organization of classes. I wondered if classes were instructed as a whole or whether they were instructed as groups, as was prevalent in the elementary schools (Cummings, 1980; Easely and Easely,

1979). How much individualization of instruction was there?

Students' behavior. How well behaved were Japanese students? Did they come to class on time? Did they respond when called on?

Teachers technique of teaching. Was the teacher a "drillmaster?" Did he demand unremitting attention and obedience? Did he explain concepts, skills, and generalization? How?

The curriculum. What was the curriculum? How were individual differences attended to? Was the curriculum spiraled? Or was mastery of materials expected when first introduced? Were different areas of mathematics (i.e., algebra, geometry, statistics) integrated, or were they taught as distinct topics and courses?

Technology. What was the role of computers and calculators in the mathematics classrooms? Was the abacus obsolete?

As I observed teachers and classes, a regularity about instruction began to emerge. It was not something that I was searching for but rather it just evolved from my observations. It was not anything I could point to and say "that's what I mean." However, I began to verbalize it for the first time after observing classes for nearly two months. A question raised by a Japanese colleague precipitated the verbalization. He asked me, "What do you see as a major difference between mathematics instruction in Hawaii as compared to Japan?" My response was, "Japanese teachers seem to teach more." Exactly what that statement entailed was to be a focal point of my observations from then on. I also began to discuss this hunch of a possible significant difference between Japanese and Hawaii teachers with a few Japanese colleagues who had also observed classes in the United States. They too intuitively sensed this difference. At this point, I started to think about what this conjecture meant and whether or not it was true throughout Japan. Were my observations thus far based on a biased sample?

Upon my return from Japan I discussed this with a colleague and started to study the research and literature on the quality of instruction and of mathematics instruction in particular. This study of the literature led me to the model of effective instruction by Good and others (Good et al., 1980). This model along with other "effective teaching" literature provided me a basis for developing an instrument "to measure" what was occurring in Japan's classrooms as compared to Hawaii's classrooms. Because the Second International Study of Mathematics (IEA, 1984) also used items about classroom processes, selected items from that study were also incorporated into the instrument I developed. What finally ensued was a survey to compare various aspects of mathematics education in Hawaii and Tokyo middle schools. This survey was facilitated in Japan by the cooperation and support of the National Institute for Educational Research and Japanese colleagues interested in mathematics education. The University of Hawaii Research Council provided general and travel support, thereby making it possible for me to discuss the analysis of the survey results with mathematics education researchers in Japan. The survey compared teacher background, teacher instructional behavior, teaching load, use of time, teacher's relative emphasis of mathematics instructional objectives, and the use of calculators in the classroom. The results of the complete survey may be found in the final report of the study (Whitman et al., 1986). In *Educational Studies in Mathematics* (Whitman & Lai, 1992) are the results about the similarities and differences in teachers' beliefs about effective teaching of mathematics. Significant mean differences between Tokyo and Hawaii teachers' classroom behavior are shown in Table 1.

Table 1
Significant Mean Differences Between Tokyo and Hawaii Teachers' Classroom Behavior

	Tokyo			Hawaii			
Item	N	x̄	SD	N	x̄	SD	t
Outline the lesson before proceeding	67	2.0	0.9	71	3.0	1.0	5.77**
Explain concepts, definitions, relationships of task to goals	67	2.2	0.7	71	1.6	0.7	-4.79

Item	N	$\bar{x}$	SD	N	$\bar{x}$	SD	t
Illustrate how to do the work, how to do the problem, etc.	66	1.6	0.6	71	1.2	0.4	-4.28
Answer students' questions about what they are to do	67	1.5	0.7	71	1.3	0.5	-2.12
Tell students to attend to tasks (whole class or individually)	67	1.6	0.8	70	2.0	0.8	2.69**
Signal students to get to work (turn off lights, eye contact, etc.	65	4.6	1.1	71	2.1	0.9	-14.53**
Encourage students to keep up (maintain pace)	66	2.2	0.9	71	1.9	0.7	-2.23*
Scan the room to see if everyone is working	67	1.2	0.4	71	1.6	0.6	4.99**
Review the students' work when it is completed	66	3.1	1.0	71	1.6	0.6	-10.49**
Monitor students' responses	67	1.3	0.6	70	1.8	0.7	4.67**
Roam the room checking students' work	67	1.4	0.6	71	2.0	0.7	5.35**
Question students: learned a concept, learned a fact, completed work	67	2.3	1.0	70	2.0	0.7	-2.02*

Item	N	x̄	SD	N	x̄	SD	t
Collect students work	67	2.5	0.8	71	1.4	0.7	-8.68**

* p< .05. ** p< .01
1: Always 2: Frequently 3: Sometimes 4: Occasionally 5: Never

As can be seen in Table 1, Tokyo teachers more than Hawaii teachers: (1) presented instruction and/or information by outlining the lesson before proceeding, (2) established and maintained the engagement of students in instruction, tasks, and activities by telling students to attend to tasks (whole class or individually), (3) monitored students' progress in learning and completing tasks by scanning the room to see if everyone is working, by monitoring students' responses, and by roaming the room checking students' work. On the other hand, Hawaii teachers: (1) explained concepts, definitions, relationship of tasks to goals, etc.; illustrated how to do the work, how to do a problem, etc.; and answered students' questions about what they are to do, (2) signaled students to get to work (turning off lights, eye contact, etc.) and encouraged students to keep up (maintain pace), (3) reviewed students' work when completed, questioned students on whether they completed work, learned a concept, or learned a fact, and collected students' work.

Middle Schools of Japan:
Kitamachi Middle School and Keio Chutoba School

Physical Appearance

Kitamachi Middle School is located in Nerima Ward situated in the northeasterly section of Tokyo (see Figure 1). It is one of 644 public middle schools in Tokyo (1983 data). Its land area encompasses 14,267 square meters. The physical plant includes a four-story concrete building, a gymnasium, and a swimming pool. The four-storied building with a floor area of 5,731 square meters has twenty-four regular classrooms and ten special classrooms for science, industrial arts, music, homemaking, and the library. In addition, it contains the offices for teacher and principal, a cafeteria, a health room and other rooms for the support and maintenance of the school. The open area (see Figure 2) is where school assemblies, physical education class activities, and play during recess occurs.

There is nothing impressive or inviting about the appearance of the school. In this regard, it looks very much like the middle schools I have frequented in Hawaii. As one enters the building, you see a series of wooden lockers where students and teachers store their outdoor shoes and those that are worn inside the school building. This is also where guests exchange their shoes for slippers. Flanking the entry hall are "security" rooms where one obtains assistance in finding one's way in the school. The teachers' room (Figure 2, Room 209), the principal's room (Figure 2, Room 207), and the clerical staff's office (Figure 2, Room 206) are on the second floor. Certain rooms are designated students' homeroom (see Figure 2, Room 108, 203-204, 303-308, 310-312, 403-408). The walls of these rooms all contain chalkboards and bulletin boards. Cubby holes where students leave their gym clothes and a storage cupboard are in the back of the room. Students have individual desks and chairs. The desks all have a hook for the students to hang their school bags, thereby freeing the desk top for class work. Each classroom has about forty desks and chairs arranged in columns of nine each. One side of the classroom contains windows that look out into the school's open area. There are white cafe-like curtains on the windows to block out sunlight and the distracting activities on the playground. During the winter months, in addition to the teacher's desk at the front of the room, there is a huge oil heater. Except for classes like music and physical education, students remain in their homeroom for instruction. It is the teacher who moves from classroom to classroom. Instead of having a room for each teacher, as is common in the United States, teachers at Kitamachi Middle School share a common teachers' room. The desks are clustered together with the vice-principal's desk at the head of the room facing the teachers.

Keio Chutobu School is located in the central part of Tokyo. It is one of 185 private middle schools in Tokyo (1983). Although it is one of the most prestigious middle schools in Japan, its physical appearance is very similar to that of Kitamachi Middle School. As is the pattern in public middle schools, students at Keio are also assigned homerooms. Each homeroom has forty-five to fifty students. In comparison to class sizes in the United States (about twenty-five each), class sizes in both public and private schools in Japan are large.

The Students

In contrast to the drab appearance of the school building were the friendly faces of the students of Kitamachi Middle School. They waved and greeted you as you approached their school, and when you left they hung out the windows wishing you their last fond "Sayonara." Kitamachi Middle School, in 1983, had 820 students, 439 boys and 381 girls (see Table 2).

Table 2
Grade Distribution of Students at Kitamachi Middle School, 1982-83.
N=820

	Boys	**Girls**	**Total**
Grade 7	137	120	257
Grade 8	141	134	275
Grade 9	161	127	288
Total	439	381	820

The grade seven class was divided into six sections, the grade eight and the grade nine class into seven each. The average section size for grade seven was forty-three, for grade eight, thirty-nine and for grade nine, forty-one. Students were grouped into sections without regard to their academic ability. This absence of ability grouping is public policy in Japan. This policy is designed to provide equal educational opportunity for all students. In the United States grouping by ability is viewed as "providing for the maximum development of each student."

Since Kitamachi is a public middle school, students attending that school lived within its vicinity. The students at Keio, a private school, came from various wards and prefectures and from above average socio-economic backgrounds. By comparison, the students at Kitamachi came from middle class homes.

Since the Postwar Occupation in 1949, education in Japan has been compulsory for grade one through nine. There is no tuition cost, and textbooks are provided by the government at no cost. However, students may be required to purchase supplementary books. For example, students buy drill and homework books for mathematics classes. Students attending Keio Chutobu School pay a tuition fee. The annual cost is approximately $2,250 (1983 data). However, textbooks for students at Keio Chutobu School also are provided free by the government.

The students at Kitamachi all wore a dark blue uniform. At Keio, the students were not required to wear uniforms. However, the girls voted to wear uniforms, and the boys chose to wear the same color as the girl's uniforms. It appears that students like to wear uniforms for group identity. While uniforms may not be required at some of the schools in Japan, the requirements of wearing a school pin continues. This serves as a means of identification of the pupils' schools when they are in the community.

Fewer of the students in the private school were inattentive in class compared to the students in the public school. In the public school, about 10% of the students showed signs of being inattentive. For example, they would read comic books, visit with each other, and observe the activities on the playground. This difference in student behavior in a public school versus that in a prestigious private school can also be seen in the United States. Undoubtedly, the selection criteria for private school students has a bearing on this difference in both Japan and the United States.

The students at both Keio and Kitamachi schools took notes diligently throughout the class period. This skill at note taking was seen at all the schools visited. According to Cummings' (1980) observations which were verified by informants, this ability was developed during their primary school years. In contrast, in the United States, only a minority, if any, of middle school students take notes throughout the class period.

Once a student of a grade level is sectioned into a particular class, he remains with that group for many other school activities. In various contests, he is identified as a member of his class team. For example, a student of class A will belong to team A in the school's sports events. Contests are among teams, not among individuals. Likewise, prizes are awarded to groups rather than individuals. Through these varied group activities, the students develop a strong group identity. They learn to place the good of the group before their individual needs.

The school groups also have lunch together in their homerooms. At Kitamachi the food is brought up to the floor of the classroom via a dumb waiter. The students set up the pots and dish out individual servings. After lunch the students also clean up. Although not required, students tend to remain together as a group between classes and during lunch recess. This group structure in the schools reflects one of the characteristics of Japanese society. In this society, the group commands the loyalty of the individual; acts are performed for the good of the group, be it the family or some other group, such as one's class.

The Use of Time

The students at Kitamachi and Keio, like the rest of the students in Japan, go to school year round. The school year begins in April and ends in March. It is made up of three terms, each of which is followed by a vacation period. The first term begins about the first week in April and ends about the third week of July followed by approximately forty days of summer vacation (about July 21 till August 31). The second term begins early in September and ends about December 25 followed by thirteen days of winter vacation (about December 26 till January 7). The last term begins about the second week in January and ends around the third week of March followed by ten days of spring vacation (about March 2 till April 5). In addition to summer, winter, and spring vacation, the schools also celebrate twelve holidays: New Year's Day (January 1), Adults' Day (January 15), National Founding Day (February 11), Vernal Equinox Day (March 21), Emperor's Birthday (April 29), Constitution Memorial Day (May 3), Children's Day (May), Respect for the Aged Day (September 15), Autumnal

Equinox Day (about September 23), Health-Sports Day (October 10), Culture Day (November 3), and Labor Thanksgiving Day (November 3).

In comparison to the United States, the number of vacation days in Japan is smaller during the summer recess, about the same during the winter recess, and greater during the spring recess. To account for the difference in school days, about 240 in Japan compared to about 180 in the United States, one needs to analyze the use of time during the school week. In Japan, the school week is from Monday through Saturday. At Kitamachi, the school day started at 8:15 a.m. for the teachers and at 8:30 a.m. for the students. Formal instruction ended at 2:20 p.m. Informal instruction ended at 3:50. However, it was not uncommon for students to remain in school until 5:00 p.m. and until 6:00 p.m. during the summer. In fact, at Kitamachi, students had to be reminded formally that they must leave the premises by 5:00 p.m. On Saturdays, formal instruction ended at 12:50 p.m., and school ended at 1:05 p.m. Instruction on Saturdays and fewer vacation days both account for the greater number of days students are in school in Japan as compared to students in the United States.

At Keio Chutobu School, the school week was also five and a half days long, and the calendar for the school year was essentially the same. The typical school day at Kitamachi was divided up as shown in Table 3.

Table 3
Time Allocation for a Typical School Day at Kitamachi

8:30-8:40	Morning meeting
8:45-8:55	Homeroom
9:00-9:45	Period 1 Formal instruction
9:55-10:40	Period 2 Formal instruction
10:50-11:35	Period 3 Formal instruction
11:45-12:30	Period 4 Forman instruction

12:30-1:00	Lunch
1:00-1:30	Recess
1:35-2:20	Period 5 Formal instruction
2:20-2:40	Homeroom
2:40-3:00	Clean up
3:00-3:45	Clubs, students meetings & activities

Formal instruction consisted of five periods of 45 minutes each. Between periods 1 through 4, students had a 10 minute recess during which they were extremely talkative and playful. Some went to the teacher's room for help; some went onto the playgrounds, while others relaxed in their classrooms.

Since the students did not move from one classroom to other between classes (the teacher moves from one location to another), the ten minutes of recess allowed students to "clear their minds," if necessary, or to "change their bearings" before proceeding with the subject of the next class. At the same time, it allowed the teachers opportunity to complete the point they were making in class. Students at both Kitamachi and Keio generally did not prepare to leave class before the bell rang. In fact, occasionally they sat right through the bell, sometimes as much as five minutes, if the teacher was still instructing. This student behavior was more prevalent at Keio than at Kitamachi school.

After lunch (12:30-1:00), students had a half hour reecess, which usually was longer since lunch was served and eaten in less than half an hour. During the lunch period, the students rearranged their furniture to form several rectangular tables to seat four or more students. One group even brought a table cloth to cover their table. The teacher rotated the table at which she sat. In this way the teacher was able to develop a personal, in addition to an academic relationship with her students. She also modeled appropriate behavior for the students at the "dining table," for example, stating "itadaki-mas," meaning "let's eat," prior to beginning a meal.

Informal instruction consists of homeroom meetings, student meetings by grades, club meetings, and drill activities. As seen in Table 3, some of these activities lasted only 10 minutes; hence, the students had to be efficient in their use of time. On Mondays, at Kitamachi, the schedule was slightly modified. As a group, the student body met outdoors from 8:30 until 8:45. At this time the goals for the week are set by the faculty and student body leaders. This was one of the means by which the students communicated with the school administration. Comments pertaining to school behavior and immediate school plans (for example, plans for school clean-up day) might be discussed. Also, school visitors were introduced, and they addressed the student body.

In addition to informal and formal instruction at Kitamachi school, students were responsible for cleaning their rooms before the start of club activities. Twenty minutes were allotted for this activity.

A major difference between the way the school day is divided for instruction in Japan as compared to the United States is that in the United States, numerous ways are used in dividing the day's time, whereas in Japan the pattern is fairly consistent. While the Ministry of Education does not provide guidelines, it does prescribe a minimum standard of instructional time for each course of study. For example, a total of 105, 140, and 140 hours (fifty-minute periods) of mathematics instruction is required for grades seven, eight, and nine respectively. Even between private and public schools, where one is most likely to see a difference, very little variation exists.

In the United States one could see a school day divided into three, four, five, or six periods. The length of the class period is usually longer than forty-five minutes. Some may be as long as 103 minutes. Generally there are five minutes of passing time from class to class. Some schools have a morning recess of fifteen to twenty minutes. Students in the United States also have about twenty minutes of homeroom in the morning where attendance and other record keeping matters are handled. In the United States, club and other extra curricula activities such as sports are elective activities and only a fraction of the student body participates, whereas in the Japan the extra curricula activities are part of the regular curricula. Students are required to participate in these activities since they are part of the school's regular program. In this respect, the middle school in Japan appears to place more effort in developing the "whole" person and not just the person's academic abilities. A teacher commented that because of past problems with violence in the schools, the teacher finds it necessary to spend more time with the students, especially in the club activities.

Although Japanese students are at school longer for a given day (8:30-3:50) than United States students, the amount of time spent by both groups in academic activities is very similar. The difference is seen in the amount of time spent in non-academic activities. In the United States the non-academic activities are optional whereas in Japan those activities are seen as part of the total required curriculum.

The Curriculum at Kitamachi

The students at Kitamachi took a total of ten subjects. These were Japanese, Social Studies, Mathematics, Science, Music, Art, Physical Education, Moral Education, English, and Industrial Arts or Homemaking. In addition, they participated in Morning Homeroom, Student Meetings, and Club Activities. Ninth graders could select an elective course in addition to these subjects and activities. A classroom period for formal instruction lasted forty-five minutes. The number of periods of instruction per week varied from course to course. For example, for all grades, Moral Education met once a week, and for Japanese Language the seventh graders met five times a week, and eight and ninth graders met four times a week (see Table 4).

Table 4
Number of Meeting Times Per Week of Courses of Study at Kitamachi Middle School, 1983

Course of Study	Grade 7	Grade 8	Grade 9
Japanese Language	5	4	4
Social Studies	4	4	3
Mathematics	3	4	4

Science	3	3	4
Music	2	2	1
Art	2	2	1
Physical Education	3	3	3
Industrial Arts or Homemaking	2	2	3
English	3	3	3
Elective	0	0	1
Moral Education	1	1	1
Homeroom and Student Meetings	1	1	1
Club Meetings	1	1	1
Total	30	30	30

The Curriculum at Keio Chutobu

The students at Keio took a total of ten subjects. These were Japanese, Social Studies, Algebra, Geometry, Science, Music, Art, Physical Education, Industrial Arts or Homemaking and English. In addition, they participated in various school activities including a school picnic, summer camp, music day, sports day, school festival, and travel for ninth graders. A class period for formal instruction lasted forty-five minutes. The number of periods of instruction per week varied from course to course. For example, for all grades English met six times a week; for music seventh and eight graders met twice a week, and ninth graders met once a week (see Table 5).

Table 5
Number of Meetings Times Per Week of Courses of Study
at Keio Chutobu School

Course of Study	Grade7	Grade 8	Grade 9
Japanese Language	6	5	5
Social Studies: Geography & History	4	5	6
Math: Algebra	3	3	2
Algebra Drill	0	0	2
Geometry	2	2	2
Science	4	4	5
Music	2	2	1
Art	2	1	1
Physical Education	3	3	3
Industrial Arts or Homemaking	1	2	0
English	6	6	6
Total	33	33	33

Some of the differences to be noted between Kitamachi and Keio schools are that in a given week, students at Keio meet more frequently for "hard core" subjects like English, Japanese, Mathematics, and Social Studies and less frequently in subjects as Art, Music, and Homemaking. Also at Keio, Moral Education and Special Activities are handled via various school activities such as camping rather than through a formalized class meeting structure. In view of the type of students attending Keio and Kitamachi schools, these differences are not surprising.

The Common Core

Central control. Although some curricula variation exist between Keio and Kitamachi middle school, both schools reflect the curriculum standards stated in the *Course of Study* issued by the Ministry of Education, Science, and Culture. The *Course of Study for Lower Secondary (Middle) School* provides the framework for curricula which each school organizes, taking into account the actual conditions of its local community and school, and the development and characteristics of its people. The *Course of Study* names three basic areas: regular subjects, moral education, and special activities. Special activities include pupils' activities (such as school assemblies and club activities), school events (such as cultural performances and school excursions), and classroom guidance on matters such as school life, use of school libraries, etc. (Ministry of Education, Science and Culture, 1982). The *Course of Study* also provides for several hours of elective subjects in which the school decides what to teach. Many schools, including Keio and Kitamachi, have chosen to teach English as an elective subject. The regular subjects prescribed are Japanese Language, Social Studies, Mathematics, Science, Music, Fine Arts, Health & Physical Education, and Industrial Arts or Homemaking. The minimum required number of school hours for each subject for each grade is shown in Table 6.

Table 6
Prescribed Subjects and Required Number of School Hours* for Lower Secondary (Middle) School**

Required Subjects	Grade 7	Grade 8	Grade 9
Japanese Language	175	140	140
Social Studies	140	140	105
Mathematics	105	105	140
Science	105	105	140

Music	70	70	35
Fine Arts	70	70	35
Health & Physical Education	105	105	104
Industrial Arts or Homemaking	70	70	105
Moral Education	35	35	35
Special Activities	70	70	70
Elective Subjects	105	105	140
Total	1,050	1,050	1,050

* A school hour is a class period of 50 minutes.
** Source: Ministry of Education, Science, & Culture, Japanese Government, 1982.

For each of the required subjects, foreign languages, moral education, and special activities, the *Course of Study* provides a set of objectives, content, suggestions for the preparation of the teaching program, and points for special consideration in teaching. The extent of the direction provided by the Ministry can be seen as one reviews the standards provided for mathematics education in grade eight in Table 7.

Table 7
Standards for Mathematics, Grades 7, 8, 9*

I. OVERALL OBJECTIVES
    To help students deepen the understanding of the basic concepts, principles, and rules concerning numbers, quantities and geometrical figures, and to enhance the ability of mathematical expression and disposition of things, thereby fostering the attitude of making use of them.
II. OBJECTIVES AND CONTENTS FOR EACH GRADE
    Second Grade (Grade 8)
    1. Objectives

(a) To help students further develop the ability to compute and transform formulas using letter symbols according to the purpose, and make use of linear equations through understanding of them.

(b) To help students further deepen and develop an awareness of viewing and considering variation and correspondence, thereby understanding the characteristics of linear functions, and also developing the ability to use them.

(c) To help students deepen the understanding of the characteristics of the basic plane figures, thereby understanding the significance and methods of mathematical inference in considering the characteristics of figures, and foster the ability of logical expression.

(d) To help students develop the ability to grasp the trends of statistical phenomena using frequency distribution, mean values, etc.

2. Contents

A. Numbers and Algebraic Expressions

(1) To enable students to do the four rules of calculation of a simple formula using letters.

(2) To help students further develop the ability to find the quantitative relationships in phenomena, and to express and apply such relationships in a formula by using letters.

(a) To make use of formulas with letters.

(b) To transform simple equalities.

(3) To help students understand the meaning of inequality and to enable them to solve a linear inequality.

(a) Meanings of inequality and its solution.

(b) To solve linear inequalities by using the properties of inequality.

(4) To help students understand the meanings of the formulation of simultaneous equations or inequalities and their solutions, thereby enabling them to solve them.

(a) Meanings of linear equation with two variables and solution.

(b) To solve simple simultaneous linear equations or linear inequalities.

B. Functions

(1) To help students further deepen the understanding of

functional relations, and develop the ability to make full use of such knowledge.

    (a) Some phenomena are described through the use of linear functions.

    (b) A linear equation with two variables is considered to express the functional relations between two variables.

(2) To help students understand the characteristics of linear functions and develop the ability to use them.

    (a) Form of the equation which expresses a linear function and the characteristics of the graph.

    (b) The ratio of changes in the values of corresponding variables of a linear function is constant.

C. Geometrical Figures

(1) To enable students to find the properties of plane figures, confirm them by using the characteristics of parallel lines and the conditions of congruence for triangles.

    (a) Displacement by parallelism, symmetry, and rotation.

    (b) Characteristics of parallel lines.

    (c) Conditions of congruence for triangles.

(2) To help students clarify the concept of similarity of figures, and develop the ability to consider the characteristics of figures by using the conditions of congruence or similarity for triangles.

    (a) Meaning of similarity, and conditions of similarity for triangles.

    (b) Characteristics of the ratio of segments of parallel lines.

    (c) Characteristics of triangles and parallelograms.

Terms and symbols: opposite angle, interior angle, exterior angle, center of gravity, R.

D. Probability and Statistics

(1) To help students collect data in accordance with the purposes, and arrange such data by using tables and graphs, and thereby enabling them to ascertain the trends of the data by paying attention to representative values, variance, etc.

    (a) Meaning of frequency distribution, and ways of looking at histogram.

    (b) Meanings of relative and cumulative frequencies.

    (c) Meanings of mean value and range.

Terms and symbols: frequency, class.

3. Points for Special Consideration in Teaching
    (1) As for Contents A(1), addition and subtraction of simple poly-
        nomials, multiplication and division of monomials, multipli-
        cation of a monomial and a polynomial, division of a polynomial
        by a monomial should be taught.
    (2) As for the "linear equations" in the contents A(4)b simultaneous
        equations with two variables should be taught.
III. PREPARATION OF THE TEACHING PROGRAM AND POINTS
     FOR SPECIAL CONSIDERATION IN TEACHING THROUGH
     ALL THREE GRADES
     A. In Grade 1 or Grade 2, a part of the contents designated for the
         grade may be briefly taught and full instruction may be given at
         the next grade so long as the objectives of the grade are
         achieved. Also, a part of the contents for the next grade may be
         taught if they do not deviate from the objectives of the specific
         grade.
     B. Terms and symbols indicated under the contents for each grade
         are for the purpose of clarifying the extent and the range of the
         contents dealt with in each grade, and therefore, in the teaching
         of such terms and symbols it is necessary to relate them to the
         contents.
     C. In teaching numerical computation of the measuring of figures
         and statistics, etc., the abacus, slide rule, or calculator should be
         used as occasion demands so as to increase the effects of
         learning.

Source: Government of Japan, Ministry of Education, Science, and
Culture (1983) *Courses of Study for Lower Secondary Schools in Japan.*
Tokyo: The Ministry.
*Grades 7, 8, and 9 are referred to as Grades 1, 2, and 3 in Japan.

Municipal control. Public middle schools, in addition to the
Course of Study, also mirror the general principles for organizing the
curriculum promulgated by the municipal board of education whose
jurisdiction they are under. For example, the Kyoto City Board of
Education in 1983 issued "The Curriculum for Kyoto City Junior High
School" (Kyoto City, BOE, 1983). It states that the curriculum for
Kyoto City Junior High Schools has been organized in accordance
with the *Course of Study*, government decrees, and the characteristics

of the city. It enumerates the following principles to be followed:

1. To bring up students with full respect for human dignity.

2. To have the students lead a balanced and meaningful school life.

3. To aim the course contents at the fundamentals which will serve as a solid basis for the growth of the student as a good citizen.

4. To promote an education in accordance with the characteristics and abilities of each student, grasping firmly the peculiar problem he has.

5. To promote an education which aims at the solution of the various problems peculiar to economically and socially segregated and underprivileged native Japanese.

6. To encourage an education based on an international point of view.

(page 6, Kyoto City, BOE, 1983)

Local implementation. Although the *Course of Study* itemizes the outlines of the aims and content of each subject, the individual schools organize, extend, and enrich the content. At Kitamachi, the teachers for each subject area met as a group at the start of the school year to organize their curriculum for the school year. These curricula were then compiled into a monograph entitled "Annual Instruction Plan for Each Subject" (Kitamachi, 1983). This monograph, in addition to being used by the teachers, is used by various committees including the Board of Education that supervises Kitamachi Middle School. In the mathematics curriculum, the plan included the months of instruction, the chapters of the text, the sections of the text, the number of days to be spent in instructing each section, the items in each section, and the description of the content of each section. Table 8 shows the organization of the eighth grade portion of the mathematics curriculum. This type of detailed and thorough curriculum planning by subject area teachers is something I have rarely seen in my more than twenty years of working with classroom teachers except perhaps at the height of school administrators desire for behavioral objectives.

Table 8

Organization of the Grade 8 Mathematics Curriculum by the Kitamachi Mathematics Teachers

The Second Grade at Kitamachi Middle Schools: Algebra

MO	Chap	Sec	Hrs	Item	Description
① April	① 1. Computation of Expressions (Formula)	1. Nominal and Polynomial Exp.	4	1. Nominal expressions and polynominal expressions	.nominal, polynominal expressions and classes (terms) / .multiplication and divisions of nominal expressions / .computation of multiplication and division
				Section Problems	
② May ③ June		2. Computation of Polynomial Expressions	10	1. Polynomia expressions / 2. Addition & subtraction of polynomial expressions / 3. Multiplication & division of polynomial and monomial expressions / 4. Application of expressions	.type of expressions (eg. binomial, trinomial) / .simplifying expressions by the distribution law / .addition & subtraction of polynomial expressions / .computation by arranging similar terms vertically / .multiplication & division of monomial and polynomial expressions / .computation of addition, subtraction, multiplication and division / .nature of multiples / .another way of expression (for the same expression)
				Section Problems	
				Chapter Problems	
④ July	② 2. Inequality	1. Inequality	8	1. Inequality & understanding its expression / 2. Nature of inequality / 3. Methods of solution of simple inequalities / 4. Application of simple inequalities	.inequality and understanding inequality / .nature of inequality / .solution of simple (linear) inequalities by using their properties / .application of simple inequalities on problems written by sentences
				Section Problems	
⑤ September		2. Simultaneous 1st-Degree Inequalities	5	1. Understanding simultaneous inequalities / 2. Solution and application of simultaneous simple inequalities	.simultaneous inequalities and its understanding / .how to solve simultaneous simple inequalities / .solve problems (sentences) by using simultaneous simple inequalities
				Section Problems	
				Chapter Problems	
⑥ October ⑦ November	③ 3. Simultaneous Equations	1. Simultaneous Equations	13	1. Understanding simple equations of two variables and simultaneous equations / 2. Methods of solving for simultaneous simple equations of two variables / 3. Various simultaneous equations / 4. Application of simultaneous simple equations of two variables	.understanding simple equations of two variables and simultaneous binary simple equations / .solve simultaneous simple equations of two variables by using the addition/subtraction and substitution methods / .solution of various simultaneous binary simple equations / eg: a. $A = B = C$ b. equations containing parenthesis c. equations consisting of fractions and decimals / .solve problems (by sentences) by using simultaneous simple equations of two variables
				Section Problems	
				Chapter Problems	

Table 8 (continued)

MO	Chap	Sec	Hrs	Item	Description
December ⑤	First Degree Functions ⑲	1. First Degree Functions	12 (7)	1. First degree functions	.meanings and expressions of first degree functions
				2. Changing values of first degree functions	.changing by constant proportion
				3. Graphs of first degree functions	.drawing graphs of first degree functions--intercepts, slopes
January ⑥			12 (5)	4. Changing area of first degree functions	.nature of the graphs of first degree functions
				5. Searching for first degree functions	.examining relationships between changing areas by drawing graphs of first degree functions
					.finding first degree functions that meet various conditions
				Section Problems	
February ⑥	4. First Degree Functions	2. First Degree Functions & Binary 1st Degree Equa.	7	1. Graphs of binomial first degree equations	.drawing binomial first degree equations
				2. Solving simultaneous binomial first degree equations by using graphs	.finding simultaneous binomial first degree equations from the intersection of lines in a graph
				Section Problems	
				Chapter Problems	
March ②		Summary	2	Exercises	.exercises①-③
					.review for one year by solving review problems①-④ etc.

Table 8 (continued)

The Second Grade at Kitamachi Middle School: Geometry

MO	Chap	Sec	Hrs	Item	Description
April ⑤	5. Parallels and Congruence ⑱	1. Parallel Lines & Angles	8	1. Angles	.classification depending upon the size of angles and nature of vertical angles
				2. Parallel lines and angles	.nature of parallel lines (parallel lines and corresponding angles; and alternate-interior angles) and conditions being parallel lines
				3. Interior and exterior angles of a triangle	.classification of triangles by angles
					relations between interior and exterior angles of triangles
					sum of interior angles of a triangle
				4. Interior and exterior angles of a polygon	.sum of interior and exterior angles of a polygon
May ⑥				Section Problems	
		2. Congruent Figures	10	1. Congruent figures	.shifting figures (parallel, rotated, symmetric) and congruence
				2. Congruent conditions for triangles	.determing the conditions for congruence of triangles
June ⑦				3. Nature of isosceles/equilateral triangles	.explaining the nature of equilateral triangles by using congruent conditions
				4. Congruence of right-angled triangles	.conditions of congruence of right-angled triangles
				Section Problems	
				Chapter Problems	
July ④	6. Parallelograms	1. Theorem & Proof ⑰	5	1. Theorem and Proof	.meaning of proof, theorem, definition, hypothesis, and conclusion; and methods of proof
				2. Another expression of the theorem	.another expression of theorem and its necessity
September ⑦				Section Problems	
		2. Parallelograms	12	1. Nature of parallelograms	.determining the nature of parallelograms from the definition and applying it
October ⑥				2. Conditions being parallelograms	.proving conditions being parallelograms and using it
				3. Particular parallelograms	.nature of rectangles, rhombuses, and squares
				4. Parallelograms and their area	.same area with different/changed shapes
				Section Problems	
				Chapter Problems	
November ⑤	7. Similar Figures ⑭	1. Similar figures	6	1. Similar figures	.meanings and expressions of similarity
					.nature, proportion, position/location and the center of similar figures
				2. Similar conditions of a triangle	.similar conditions of a triangle
December ④				Section Problems	
		2. Parallel Lines & Ratio of Segments	8 (4)	1. Parallel lines and ratios	.nature of ratios
					.triangles and ratios
					.center-point theorem (in triangles)
					.parallel lines and ratios
January ⑤				2. Center of gravities of a triangle	.center of gravities (centroid) theorem (in triangles)
				Section Problems	
				Chapter Problems	

Table 8 (continued)

NO	Chap	Sec	Hrs	Item	Description
February	⑥ Data Adjustment/ Arrangement ⑫	1. Data Adjustment	7	1. Distribution of numbers	.drawing bar graphs and line graphs from the distribution tables reading/judging its trends
				2. Relative numbers and accumulative numbers	.computation and expression of relative and accumulative numbers
				3. Representative numbers (eg: mean, median, mode)	.computations of mean, median and mode
	6.			Section Problems	
March ⑬	Summary	2		Exercises	.review for one year by solving review problems⑤-⑬

Textbooks and supplementary materials. The plan of the mathematics curriculum is built around the mathematics textbooks' organization and content. The table of contents of the textbooks are very detailed, thus allowing for the correlation of the textbook with the teachers' annual curriculum. Reproduced in Table 9 is the table of contents of the seventh grade mathematics textbook.

Table 9
Organization of Grade 7 Mathematics Textbook

Table of Contents
    A. Integers
        1. Characteristics of Integers
            (a) Integers
            (b) Prime Numbers and Prime Factors
        2. Positive and Negative Numbers
            (a) Signed Numbers
            (b) Order of Numbers (greater than and less than)
        3. Addition and Subtraction
            (a) Addition
            (b) Subtraction
            (c) Addition and Subtraction Calculations
        4. Multiplication and Division
            (a) Multiplication
            (b) Division
            (c) Four Rules for Calculating
    Chapter Problems

B. Literal Expressions
  1. Using Literal Expressions
     (a) Numbers and Variables
     (b) Rules for Using Literal Expressions
     (c) Quantitative Expressions
  2. Literal Expressions and Calculations
     (a) Substitution and Value of Expressions
     (b) Calculation of First Degree Linear Expressions
  Chapter Problems
C. Equation
  1. Equation
     (a) Equation
  2. Method of Solution of Equations
     (a) Characteristics of Equality
     (b) Characteristics of Equality and Method of Selection
     (c) Method of Solution of Linear Expressions
     (d) Application of Linear Expressions
  Chapter Problems
D. Function and Proportion
  1. Variation and Function
     (a) Variable
     (b) Function
  2. Proportion and Inverse Proportion
     (a) Proportion
     (b) Inverse Proportion
  3. Coordinate and Graph
     (a) Coordinate
     (b) Graph of Function
  Chapter Problems
E. Plane Figures
  1. Straight Line and Circle
     (a) Straight Line and Angle
     (b) Circle and Sector
  2. Construction and Set of Points
     (a) Fundamental Construction
     (b) Set of Points and Figures
  Chapter Problems

F. Solid Figures
    1. Solid Figures
        (a) Line and Plane Relationships
        (b) Polyhedra
        (c) Some Different Points of View
    2. Surface Area and Volume
        (a) Prism, Circular Cylinders
        (b) Pyramid, Circular Cone, Sphere
    Chapter Problems
    Calculation Exercises
    Review Problems
    Index

Source: Kunihiko et al. Atarashii Suugaku 1 (New Mathematics)

In comparison to American textbooks, Japanese textbooks are very small. For example, the mathematics textbooks at Kitamachi school were 15cm by 21cm and contained about 175 pages. They are soft-covered. The textbooks contain the essential mathematical ideas and skills that the students are expected to learn. In Figure 3 are two sample pages from the grade eight textbook. On these pages are found the complete coverage of the topics of angles and vertical angles in the middle mathematics series. See Figure 4 for the translation of these two pages.

As can be seen in Figure 4, Japanese mathematics textbooks contain very few drill and practice problems as compared to their American counterparts. Probably this is why the students are asked to buy drill books and homework books. Another difference is that American textbooks attempt to provide a variety of materials so that teachers may individualize their instructions and provide for individual differences via differentiated assignments. In Japan, because the classroom teacher is expected to provide a basic core of knowledge to all students, he does not individualize his instruction. Providing everyone with the same instructions assures (so it is believed) equal educational opportunities for all students, whereas individualized instructions suggest unequal educational opportunities.

Textbooks are provided free of charge to students in public and private schools in grades one through nine by the Minister of Education, Science, and Culture. In the United States, textbooks are loaned to the students in public schools. They are not expected to purchase any supplementary texts, such as workbooks. Private school students generally buy their books and any needed supplementary materials.

At Kitamachi school, the seventh, eighth, and ninth grade mathematics classes use exactly the same mathematics textbooks as are used by the same grade levels of the other thirty-one middle schools of Nerima Ward. Every three years, all of the thirty-two schools vote for the textbook they wish to use for the next three years. The textbook with the greatest number of votes is chosen. The mathematics teachers of each school review the textbooks that are approved by the Ministry of Education and that are displayed at the textbook exhibition. Teachers then decide for which text their school will vote.

The Ministry of Education, Science and Culture authorizes textbooks for school use for all elementary and secondary schools. Before a textbook is authorized, the Minister consults with the textbook Authorization and Research Council. Members of this Council are appointed from among teachers and other learned persons by the Minister. Before the Council makes its recommendations to the Minister, it reviews the results of separate part-time textbook examiners in the Council and of full-time specialists in the Ministry. On the basis of the Council's recommendation, the Ministry authorizes textbooks. A list of authorized textbooks is sent to the prefecture boards for their textbook selection.

At Keio school, as is the case with all private schools, the principal adopts textbooks from the list authorized by the Ministry. He receives information and advice from the Metropolitan Tokyo Prefectural Board of Education.

On the other hand, textbook publication and adoption is very varied in the United States. At the middle school level, generally each teacher decides which textbook to use, if he decides to use a textbook at all. A survey conducted in the State of Hawaii (Whitman, 1975) revealed that as many as fifty-three mathematics textbooks or programs were used in the seventh grade and as many as sixty in the eighth grade. In 1982, Japan authorized about six middle school mathematics series for adoption. In the United States, various states attempt to control the quality of textbooks used by approving textbooks for adoption. In large states, such as California and Texas, that provide free textbooks, control is the greatest. In fact, these states indirectly control what will be published since adoption in any of these states means extremely large sales for textbook publishers; hence, they will cater to these states. In a small state such as Hawaii that does not provide free textbooks, control is very limited even when an approved list of textbooks is issued. In the Hawaii survey cited above (Whitman, 1975) of the 7th grade books used, 72 % were not on the approved list and of the 8th grade books used, 78 % were not on the approved list.

Although the textbook at Kitamachi school was of paramount importance, other materials were used to obtain the objectives of the school program (one of the reasons being that the textbooks contained only the minimal essentials relative to content). For example, in mathematics instruction, sufficient material was lacking for reinforcing, maintaining, and applying the skills and concepts learned. Hence, students were assigned additional work from a supplementary workbook. As seen in Figure 5, the workbook consisted of problems to be solved, following a sample problem and solution. Figure 6 contains the translation of Figure 5. In the United States much of this kind of material is found in the regular textbook. This, in part, may account for the large size of the United States textbook.

In addition to the workbook, students also used a drill book. As seen in Figure 7 (see Figure 8 for its translation), this book consists only of drill type problems to develop algebraic computational skills. Students practiced on drill problems in their 10-minute morning meeting class. This morning meeting class was used to practice all types of drill materials, not only mathematics. Students drilled themselves without teacher assistance.

Teachers at Kitamachi and Keio schools also developed supplementary materials called "printo" to assist their students. These "printo" varied in content. They included glossaries, summaries of key concepts and generalizations, and problems for application. A sample summary "printo sheet" by one of the Kitamachi teachers is shown in

Figure 9. The translation of it is in Figure 10. Teachers at these schools also wrote their own quizzes and examinations. In both Japan and the United States, teachers in order to do their best teaching find it necessary to develop supplementary materials for their students.

Inside the Classroom

At both Kitamachi and Keio schools the class periods were forty-five minutes long. Because students remained in the same classroom for various subjects and because there was a ten-minute recess between periods, students were already in class when the teacher arrived. All classes began with a greeting and a bow by teachers and students. This, rather than the bell, signaled the start of instruction. Likewise a bow and saying "sayonara" (good-bye) signaled the period's end. The attention given to this ritual was performed by students varied from teacher to teacher. Some expected the full attention of all students, others allowed some students to be inattentive. One teacher commented to me on the difficulty she had imagining a class without an "opening" or "closing" to the period as it is customary in America.

The teachers generally taught the class as a whole. They devoted much time to explaining and/or demonstrating the new concepts, generalizations, and skills. Time was also assigned to guiding students in learning and practicing the ideas presented. Frequently this was done by walking around the room and observing whether students were progressing satisfactorily on work given by the teacher after the explanation and/or demonstration. This was also done by having groups of students working at the blackboard as well as at their seats, or individual students might come before the class to explain and/or demonstrate a proof, skill, or idea.

As I observed classes in Tokyo and Kyoto, one major difference stood out in my mind: Japanese teachers seemed to place more energy than teachers in Hawaii into teaching the subject matter. The quality of instruction seemed greater there than what I've observed in Hawaii. As I tried to delineate the differences in terms of specific behavior, I learned of the model of effective mathematics teaching by Good, Grouws, & Ebmeier (1983). The model states that time devoted to developing a mathematics lesson would improve the performance of students on standardized achievement tests. Furthermore, development which utilizes about 50% of the class time was described in terms of the following teacher behavior:

1.   Review briefly and/or identify prerequisite skills.

2.   Focus upon the development of meaning and comprehension using active demonstration and teacher exploration.

3.   Assess student comprehension (ask questions/work on supervised practice).

4.   Repeat meaning portion of the lesson as necessary (using different examples and explanations if possible).

5.   Provide practice opportunities for students:

     (a)   Practice should be short (one or two problems at a time).

     (b)   Students should be held responsible for assigned practice problems.

     (c)   Practice should be performed in a meaningful context (teacher provides frequent process explanations).

     (d)   When success rate is high, move students into seat work portion of the lesson, where students have an opportunity for uninterrupted practice.

(pp. 35-36, Good et al., 1983)

As I review the video tapes of classroom instruction in Japan and of the classroom notes taken, I am struck by the amount of class time the Japanese teachers devoted to "developing a lesson" as described by Good, et al. More than 50% of the class time was used to develop a lesson. On many days, more than 75% of class time was so used. Details of some of their techniques of development will be described later in the book. Japanese teachers were able to spend the amount of time they do on lesson development because they considered it of utmost importance.

In the classroom, students were encouraged and willingly presented their mathematical arguments. On one occasion, a student explained a solution that the teacher had not seen. She applauded this effort and suggested his classmates likewise applaud. On another occasion, as many as six students came before the class to demonstrate the supposed validity of their arguments. The first five realized, as did their classmates, the fallacy of their arguments as they proceeded. The class spontaneously cheered the student who finally presented a valid argument. In this classroom atmosphere where logical reasoning is stressed, the student was also willing to challenge the teacher's word although whenever a student did so, his classmates teased him.

At Kitamachi, I noted that the class with the greatest amount of students not on task were those of a beginning teacher. The class with the least amount (many times none at all) of students not on task were the ninth-grade classes. The eighth grade classes generally had about 10% of students not on task. Students who were not on task did the following:

1. Look out the windows onto the playgrounds;
2. Draw pictures;
3. Read comics or other non-academic materials;
4. Hide in the closet;
5. Throw chalk in the air; and
6. Visit with one another.

Either the teachers did not see these misbehaviors, or they chose to ignore them. In all classes, students who did not remain on task were generally ignored by the other students. The 10% of students not on task were not the same ones every day. On one day, a student would be inattentive most of the period; on other days, he might be immersed in the class lesson. Those who tended to be inattentive, however, tended to come from a definite sub-group of about ten students. Also, the students who tended to be inattentive were not those whose achievement was the lowest.

At the private school, generally all the students were on task. When they were not, they were usually visiting with each other. These students tended to be the same ones and were noted by the teachers.

Compared to teachers in American classrooms, the Japanese teachers spent less time attending to keeping order in the classroom. What is not clear is whether there actually is a great difference in classroom behavior, or whether American teachers tend to react more readily to those individuals who are not exhibiting the desired behavior. Because American teachers are trained to teach each individual to his maximum potential, whereas Japanese teachers emphasize the need to reach the greatest numbr of students, the Japanese teacher will tend to concentrate on the great majority. Also, mathematics classes in the United States are generally homogeneously grouped by ability and achievement, and hence weaker and more troublesome students tend to be in the same classroom, thereby magnifying disorder. Because all are weak in the subject matter, it is not difficult for one student to distract the other. In comparison, in Japan, because the students are randomly placed in a class, there are likely to be only a few weak and/or troublesome students in a given class. In fact, these few will find it difficult to adversely influence the rest of the class. The other students are good role models for the weaker students, and they help to channel those students' behavior in a positive direction.

Another possible reason for less student disturbance in the classroom is that students are involved in instruction. They are under the guidance of the teacher nearly all the time. They practice doing problems on their own after having been led through the developmental phase of the lesson. Hence, the likelihood of their being successful on the assigned work is greatly enhanced, thereby avoiding frustrating moments and occasions to misbehave. The role of planning to improve classroom management has been recognized (Emmer, et al., 1984). The model by Good, et al., recognizes the role of planning and further delineates the substance of the classroom momentum. I have only discussed the developmental phase of their plan since it is this phase of the model that dominates the Japanese mathematics classroom.

In both, the public and private schools observed, no students were seen using an abacus, calculator, or computer. One of the private school teachers was studying computers and their feasibility for classroom instruction. In Tokyo some of the middle schools forbade the use of calculators in class (Whitman, 1986). However, the *Course of Study* for the middle schools encourages the use of the abacus, slide rule, or calculator in the classroom to increase the effects of learning when dealing with numerical computations, when studying measurement, statistics, etc. (Ministry of Ed., page 43, 1983). In comparison to Japan, in the United States, calculators and computers are more widely utilized in the classroom. The computers are used in various areas of study including English composition, science, and mathematics.

Outside the Classroom

Homework. Instruction in mathematics and other subjects occurs not only in school, but also in the home and *juku*. Parental attitudes toward mathematics have a strong, positive influence on student attitudes (Imai Toshihiro, 1984). This is a major reason for the success of Japanese students in learning mathematics. (This is suggested by Sawada Toshio, director of the Science Educational Research Center, National Institute for Education Research, Tokyo, Japan, in a private communication, on November 30, 1987). Students not only discuss school with their parents, but also seek help in doing homework. When asked who helps you with mathematics homework, of the seventh graders, 26% said their parents helped, and of the eighth graders 15% said their parents helped. In addition to seeking help from their parents, students also sought the help of their older siblings. For seventh graders this amounted to 15% and for eighth graders 16%. However, the *juku* teacher was the person most sought for help. 40% of seventh graders and 47% of eighth graders sought his help (Sawada & Sachino, 1986).

In comparison with United States mathematics classrooms, little to no time in Japanese classrooms appeared to be allotted to doing newly assigned homework. In fact, in piloting a questionnaire at Keio school, the students were puzzled by the question, "choose the percent of class time the teacher has students working on new homework: 0%; 25%; 50% 100%." It seemed to them very contradictory to speak of homework as being done in class. Of the forty-eight students in the class, the most common choice was 0%. Not infrequently in my observations of mathematics classes in Hawaii, classroom instruction appeared to revolve around the homework. Teachers would admonish, "You had best pay attention in class so you can do the homework." Invariably, instruction began with the correction of the previous day's homework. The teacher worked out the problems that students found difficult. This might take as long as thirty minutes and in a few cases nearly forty-five minutes. During the last twenty minutes of the class period, the students would be assigned to begin their homework. This focus was also noted by Welch (Stake and Easely, 1978) in his classroom observations.

At Kitamachi, my host teacher placed the homework assignment on the bulletin board with its due date. Homework was assigned a week in advance and was collected every Tuesday. The teacher collected and corrected the assignments.

When I asked my host teacher at Keio school how he handled homework, he replied that he assigned homework in the workbook. Since answers are provided, students correct their own work. As a check, he gave a quiz once a week. He added, "there really is no time in class for correcting homework." He reflects a commonly held belief among Japanese mathematics teachers that they should use class time to present the subject matter. In a questionnaire (Whitman et al., 1986), 94% of Japanese mathematics teachers surveyed rated this activity of most or greatest importance. Also, there is the belief that Japanese students learn by hearing the teachers' explanation as compared to reading the textbook (Sugiyama, 1986). One teacher explained that there was not much to be read in the textbook. In Hawaii, more commonly I would hear the teacher comment, "The homework correction took too long, so I didn't have enough time to present the new material."

The relatively small amount of mathematics homework given (Whitman, et al., 1986, Sawada & Kobayashi, 1986) and the limited amount of attention paid to it could be partly attributed to the influence of the *juku* (after school) classes that about 50% of the students attend.

Juku. The frequency with which seventh and eighth graders attended *juku* is shown in Table 10. Regardless of grade level, students most frequently attended *juku* twice a week for a period of two hours.

Table 10
Frequency of *Juku* Attendance and Number of Hours at *Juku*, 1984
N=1811

	Percent of Students	
	Gade 7	Grade 8
Number of Days/Week		
1	30	38
2	49	44
3	14	15
4	06	01
Greater than		
5	01	02
Number of Hours/Visit		
1	13	13
2	47	62
3	20	14
4	09	07
5	05	01
6	04	03
Greater than		

7	02	00

* Based on data in "An Analysis of the Effect of Arithmetic and Mathematics Education at *Juku*," Sawada Toshio and Kobayashi Sachino (National Institute for Educational Research, Tokyo, 1986)

The Teachers, Teacher Education, and Workload

At Kitamachi there were five mathematics teachers; three were full-time teachers, and one was a part-time teacher. All three of the full-time teachers held regular first class teacher certificates for the lower secondary (middle) school in mathematics teaching. Nearly all of the other full-time teachers held regular certificates for lower secondary school. These certificates are for specified subject areas and are valid for all prefectures and for life. They are granted by prefectural boards of education. To obtain a regular first class certificate, teachers minimally need a Bachelor's degree (120 credit hours), including thirty-six credit hours in general education, forty or thirty-two credit hours in the teaching specialty, depending on the specialty, and fourteen hours of professional subjects including theory of pedagogy, pedagogical psychology, and teaching methods. For the second class certificate, teachers need minimally two years beyond upper secondary school (sixty-two credit hours) including eighteen credit hours in general education, twenty or sixteen hours in the teaching specialty, and ten credit hours in professional subjects. More particularly, the program of studies for one of the teachers observed who taught at the private school and had a first class lower secondary school certificate is seen in Table 11.

Table 11
Program of Studies for a Private School Teacher: First Class Lower Secondary Certificate

Subject	Credits **or Units**
General **Education**	
Ethics	4

Psychology	4
Logic	4
Law	4
Politics	4
Economics	4
Sociology	4
Mathematics	4
Physics	4
Chemistry	4
English A	4
English B	4
Health Education and Hygiene	1
Theory of Physical Ecuation	1
Training	2
Teaching Speciality Professional	
Analysis I	4
Algebra I	4
Geometry I	4
Analysis II	5
Algebra II	5
Geometry II	5
Mathematical Statistics I	5

Junior Course of Seminar	6
Senior Course of Seminar	10
Functions of a Complex Variable	4
General Topology	4
Numerical Analysis	4
Mathematics for Education	4
Modern Higher Algebra	4
Surveying	2
Fundamentals of Education	4
Educational Psychology & Adolescence Psychology	4
Method of Teaching Mathematics	4
Method of Moral Education	2
Student Teaching Practice	2

*One credit hour is equivalent to a 15 week lecture class of one hour per week, requiring two hours of student preparation for each.

Although the prefectures in Japan grant teacher certificates, the criteria by which they are granted are standardized. This is in contrast to the situation in the United States where each state issues certificates; however, the criteria are not standardized. For example, in the state of Delaware to be certified as a secondary school mathematics teacher, the following are required: (1) Bachelor's degree from an accredited college, (2) completion of a teacher education program in mathematics or fifteen semester hours in professional education (to include human behavior, methods and materials, and clinical and/or field experience including student teaching) and (3) thirty semester hours of specific mathematics courses. On the other hand, in Hawaii the requirements are (1) completion of a five-year teacher education program at a state approved institution, (2) completion of a graduate teacher program at a state approve institution, or (3) completion of two years of successful teaching in the public schools of Hawaii (Woellner, 1983).

The teachers at Kitamachi school were appointed by the prefectural board of education. Prior to appointment, the teachers took an appointment examination that included both the subject area of instruction and professional subjects. Since all the teachers had teacher certificates, they qualified for appointment. Because Kitamachi is a municipal school, these teachers were recommended by the municipal board of education to the prefectural board for appointment.

The three regular mathematics teachers at Kitamachi had twenty-eight, sixteen, and no years of service. The one with twenty-eight years of experience taught four classes of the same subject for a total of sixteen teaching hours; in addition he supervised a homeroom, the table tennis club and two student meetings, and served on the culture and exhibition committees. The teacher with sixteen years of experience taught four ninth grade level mathematics classes for a total of sixteen teaching hours. These classes covered the same subject matter. The teacher also had other responsibilities. In particular, he was a ninth grade homeroom teacher and had to make recommendations to students as to which high school they might consider applying to. This recommendation was especially important because students could apply for only one public high school and must successfully pass that school's examinations to be accepted. If the student failed the high school entrance examination, he had to wait another year to reapply to that school or another public high school, or he could apply to a private high school. However, a private high school is more costly than a public high school.

The new teacher with no years of experience taught classes for a total of seventeen teaching hours. Two of these classes were eighth-grade level mathematics, and three were seventh-grade mathematics. This gave him two preparations in comparison to the one required of the other two regular mathematics teachers. Like all teachers in the school, he also had to contribute to and work on extracurricular activities and school events. The workload, in terms of subject teaching hours per week , of the mathematics teachers at Kitamachi is consistent with the statistical results obtained in a nation-wide survey conducted by the Ministry of Education, Science, and Culture (See Table 12) (NIER, 1986).

Table 12
Average Number of Teaching Hours* Per Week for Japanese
Public School Teachers, October 1983

School Level	Teaching Hours
Elementary School (1-6)	22.3
Lower Sceondary School (7-9)	16.5
Upper Secondary School (10-12)	15.2

*Subject matter teaching only. In addition to subject matter teaching, teachers usually donate their time to extra-curricular activities, school events, preparation of lessons, grading papers, etc.

In terms of student load, the most experienced teacher had 156 students, the next most experienced had 164, and the least experienced had 187.

In terms of workload, in general, what we see at the middle school level are teachers teaching one or two subjects in which they are certified. Their class size average is about forty. The total number of class contact hours is about 16 per week. These hours are distributed over five and a half days. In addition to subject matter teaching, teacher devote their time to extracurricular activities, school events, and preparation for their teaching responsibilities. The teachers are not required to be physically present in school if they have no responsibilities that require their presence. In this last respect, the Japanese teachers are treated more like college and university instructors in the United States. Middle school teachers in the United States are required to be present at the school regardless of whether or not they are instructing.

The dedication of the teachers at Kitamachi cannot be measured by official workload alone. These teachers spent much time among themselves in small work groups planning for classes and other activities. There is a high degree of collegiality among the teachers. This is a reflection of the value the Japanese place on the welfare of the group. The success of teachers is measured by the achievements of teachers collectively, not by teachers individually. Also, the fact that the teachers all share a common room as their office enhances the opportunity for group work. In the mornings, many of these teacher groups would be bustling with activity. This type of activity also occurred between classes and after school. It was not unusual to see teachers at school past the official closing time. Teachers could also be seen working or otherwise interacting with students before school, between classes, and after school. The relationship between teacher and students seemed to be very warm. The students indicated to me the "nicknames" they had coined for their teachers. One senses the endearment with which these names were given. Teachers on the other hand expressed to me their concern for the general welfare of the student. In fact, at the time of my visit, an extra effort was being made by the school to communicate to the students and to demonstrate to them the school's concern for their welfare. This endeavor was prompted by some violence experienced at the school the year before. The relationship between teacher and student seemed somewhat similar to a parent and child relationship. When a student ran into difficulties outside of school, the authorities first notified his teacher who in turn notified the parents. One of the teachers told me that sometimes he would lay awake at night thinking about his students. Another teacher indicated that the students were truly Japan's most valuable natural resource, and that the cultivation of the students' intellect was necessary for Japan's well-being. Concern for students is so high that union strikes by teachers were conducted after school so that students would not be penalized. In order for one of the homerooms to have a party in the recreation room during class hours, the teachers held a meeting so that the classes could be rearranged to accommodate the students. Concern for students was also expressed by the principal when he asked me how we handled "tom-boys" in American schools. This was a matter of great concern to him. He saw the socialization of the students as the school's responsibility. Very much like a parent, he wanted to see the girl students behave as young ladies and not "tom-boys." Some of the warmth the students had for their teachers spilled over onto me. Frequently students would come to chat with me between classes, before and after school, and during lunch recess. Their student body representatives held a meeting to 'interview" me, and the school's paper devoted a few articles to my visit. As a visitor, I felt I was gradually being made part of their school family. My comings and goings attracted much of their attention.

It is the warmth of the students and teachers that lingers in my mind when I think back to my stay at Kitamachi School.

CHAPTER 2
SECOND FIELD STUDY:
SAPPORO AND OSAKA, 1992

At this site, study focused on the middle school mathematics curriculum, specially its geometric aspects, the performance of students in geometry, and the teaching of geometry in the classroom. The study compared the geometric curriculum in the United States with that of Japan; it compared students' performance in Hawaii with that in Osaka and Sapporo, and it compared instruction in geometry in Japan and Hawaii.

Compared with my original site study, entry into the schools in Sapporo and Osaka was not a major problem. I now worked with a professor at the University of Tsukuba as part of the Japan-United States Teacher Education Consortium, the purposes of which included collaborative research between Japanese and United States educators. This professor, in turn, had colleagues at Osaka Kyoiku University and Hokkaido Education University who cooperated with us in our collaborative research projects.

The Middle School Geometry Curriculum of the United States and Japan

The analysis of the middle school curriculum was done by comparing the most recent *Course of Study* by Mombusho (Mombusho, 1989) in Japan with the Standards (NCTM, 1989) of the National Council of Teachers of Mathematics in the United States. (Although the *Revised Courses of Study* for the middle schools were implemented in 1993, they were announced in 1989.) The curriculum in the United States is promoted by the national mathematics teachers' organization, whereas in Japan it is mandated by the government.

In the United States, the "Standards for Geometry" are stated mainly in Standard 12: In grades 5-8, the mathematics curriculum should include the study of the geometry of one, two, and three dimensions in a variety of situations so students can:

(a) identify, describe, compare, and classify geometric figures;
(b) visualize and represent geometric figures with special attention to developing spatial sense;
(c) explore transformations of geometric figures;
(d) represent and solve problems using geometric models;
(e) understand and apply geometric properties and relationships;
(f) develop an appreciation of geometry as a means of describing the physical world.

In Japan "geometry" does not exist as an independent subject, but rather is integrated systematically into various parts of the mathematics curricula. Knowledge of and skills with various geometrical figures, (e.g., triangles, squares, rectangles, and circles) are intuitively studied in elementary school; the development of logical reasoning, mathematical inferences and proofs are introduced in middle school. Also, since the number of days that students attend school in Japan is greater than that in the United States, more time is devoted to the teaching of geometry.

At the middle school level, the contents include congruence and similarity, and methods of mathematical inference with demonstration or proof. In addition, work with coordinates and graphs of linear functions are included.

Essentially, the Japanese intended geometry curriculum is about two grade levels above that in the United States. The study of formal proof is intended for grade eight, whereas in the United States, the intended curriculum places the study of formal geometry that includes deductive proof at grade ten.

The Geometric Performance of Japan and Hawaii Students

Hawaii and Japan students were compared according to the distribution levels in the van Hiele theory, which postulates the existence of five levels of understanding (thinking with reference to specific topic areas in geometry). The properties of these levels as suggested by Hoffer (1985, p. 207) are as follows:

Level 0 (Visualization). Figures are judged by their appearance as a whole without regard to properties of their components.

Level 1 (Analysis). The student begins to discern the properties of figures; figures are recognized as having parts and are recognized by their parts.

Level 2 (Inference). The student logically orders the properties of concepts and figures and uses one-step deduction.

Level 3 (Deduction). The student can construct proofs, understand the role of axioms and definitions, and supply the reasons for steps in a proof.

Level 4 (Rigor). The student can understand the formal aspects of deduction and can interrelate different axiomatic systems of proof.

These levels are sequential. The student must master one level of understanding (thinking) before proceeding to the next level. Knowledge of the language structure is pertinent to the advancement in level of thinking.

Sample. Both the Hawaii and Japan students were tested in April or May, 1992. Since the Japan school year begins in April and the Hawaii school year ends in early June, the Hawaii students were tested at the end of grades eight and ten, whereas the Japanese students were tested at the beginning of grades nine and eleven.

The Hawaii sample consisted of 159 eighth graders and 159 students in grades nine through twelve, with the great majority being tenth graders. The eighth graders were selected from two schools.

About a third of the eighth graders were considered by their teachers to be average, and the remainder represented a range of ability from average-low to high-high. The tenth graders were students from three high schools. These high schools are average high schools.

Students from Sapporo, Japan made up the grade seven and grade nine samples. The students for all grade levels were average students.

Test instruments. Based on the translated writings of the van Hiele (Fuys et al., 1984) and studies by Fuys and Geddes (1984) and Usiskin (1982), three tests were developed and pilot tested in Hawaii. These tests are Geometry 1a (twenty-two items) for third/fourth graders, Geometry 2a (twenty-four items) for sixth/seventh graders, and Geometry 3a (thirty-three items) for eighth/ninth graders and for tenth/eleventh graders. Geometry 1a tested for levels 0, 1, 2 attainment; Geometry 2a tested for levels 0, 1, 2; and Geometry 3a tested for levels 0, 1, 2, 3. The geometry content of the test was that generally found in the curricula of both Japan and Hawaii. The test items with their indicated correct responses were categorized by levels.

After the tests were piloted and revised, they were sent to Japan for review and translation. A mathematics teacher in Hawaii then translated and revised the English version of the tests based on the Japanese suggestions. How the tests should be administered and scored was communicated to the Japanese. In general, the details were agreed to by both parties.

The data obtained (see Table 13) reveal a two-year gap in performance levels in middle school geometry students. Part of this difference can be accounted for by the geometry curriculum and, as will be noted later, by the instruction in verbal communication. When analyzing test items, it was also noted how language and context seem to influence how a student's response to a test item. This is especially true in cross-cultural studies.

Table 13
Percent of Correct Responses on the Van Hiele Geometry Test in Japan and Hawaii

	Japan		Hawaii	
	Grade 9	Grade 11	Grade 8	Grade 10*
Part A: Level 0	73	87	66	83
Part B: Level 1	33	66	55	74
Part C: Level 2	31	51	40	63
Part D: Level 3			04	22
# Of Students	131	113	159	159

**Grade 10 contains students in grades 10-12 who are enrolled in a conventional tenth grade geometry class.

Teaching Geometry in Japan and Hawaii

To compare geometry instruction in Japan and Hawaii relative to the appropriateness of the content and teaching strategies as they pertain to the van Hiele level of the students, the NCTM Standards, and the Mombusho Course of Study, classes in Japan and Hawaii were videotaped for analysis.

In both Japan and Hawaii the classes were studying congruence of triangles — a topic wherein the concepts and procedures of deductive reasoning and mathematical proof are introduced. Instruction lasted for thirteen days in Hawaii and eight in Japan. In Japan the students were in grade eight, and in Hawaii they were in grade ten. The students in Hawaii were average to above-average, whereas in Japan they were above average. Both teachers were experienced teachers, but the

Hawaii teacher was inexperienced as a high school teacher. Both had strong mathematics backgrounds. The class size in Japan consisted of forty students, whereas in Hawaii it consisted of thirteen students.

Videotaping was done for eleven days in Hawaii and five in Japan. Instruction on the topic of congruence of triangles took thirteen days in Hawaii and eight in Japan.

The lessons were analyzed to determine the level of thinking of a student and the phase of instruction of a teacher using a coding scheme developed by Hoffer (1994). Hoffer describes the five phases in the van Hiele model as follows:

Phase 1. Familiarization. The students become acquainted with the working domain.

Phase 2. Guided Orientation. The students uncover the links that form relationships.

Phase 3. Verbalization. The students become aware of relations that they try to express in words with increasing accuracy. Students learn the technical language of the topic.

Phase 4. Free Orientation. The students are able to find their way in a network of relations.

Phase 5. Integration. The students build an overview of the subject.

In Hawaii, the class period varied in length from thirty-eight minutes to seventy-four minutes, whereas in Japan each class period was fifty minutes long. In both Japan and Hawaii the style of instruction was whole class instruction. In Hawaii the teacher questioned students, provided information and explanations, and had students communicate their thinking to the class. In Japan, the class lessons followed a particular pattern. (I discuss this further in my observation of classes in Sapporo as the "open-ended" approach to teaching). The pattern is this:

1. The teacher reviews what the students had previously learned.

2. The teacher poses a problem.

3. The students try to solve it in 10 to 25 minutes. The teacher walks around the classroom and questions students for suggestions on how to solve the problem. Some students write and explain their answers on the chalkboard.

4. Other students and the teacher raise questions about the explanation. The teacher teaches new content, and at the same time, uses the students' approach, solution, and explanation.

5. The teacher summarizes what was learned from the process of solving the original problem.

6. The teacher usually gives some problems for homework.

Based on the analysis of the videotapes, the following differences and similarities were noted between Hawaiian and Japanese classrooms:

*   More students were functioning at level 4 in Japan than in Hawaii.

*   More teacher instruction in Japan was at phases 3 and 5 than in Hawaii. Phase 5 teaching is reflected in the summary activity of the teacher. In a previous study, summary activity by teachers was prevalent in Japanese classroom teaching (Whitman & Lai, 1990).

*   In Japan the teaching process is different. In Japan, free orientation (problem solving) is given before any explanation by the teacher. After the students work at solving the problem, the teacher and students reflect on their problem solving. Afterwards, the teacher explains the material and summarizes.

*   In Japan, the amount of time used in solving and discussing a single problem exceeds that in Hawaii.

- Both classrooms exhibited multiple phases and levels within a given module.

- The time allocations for the modules were generally the same for both classrooms.

- Both classrooms were teacher-led, and instruction was for the entire class.

- The interaction between the students and teacher seemed positive for both classes.

- Both classes, in general, followed their text for the curriculum.

- The Japanese class took fewer days (eight versus thirteen) to teach the initial concept of proof.

Classroom Observations

In 1992, both in Osaka and Sapporo, I was able to review curriculum materials that the students used and to observe classroom teaching. A total of fifteen class periods were observed involving six teachers and five schools. Based on these observations I noted some common elements across the classrooms. These I discuss below.

Communication. Oral communication of mathematical ideas and of errors flowed with ease between student and teacher and among students. The classroom atmosphere was very conducive to this kind of dialogue. The students also were able to communicate orally and in writing their mathematical thoughts in front of the entire class. The discussion of mathematics between and among students was not uncommon.

In discussion with my Japanese colleague who accompanied me to all the classes visited, I learned that the Japanese philosophy of teaching encourages much classroom discourse. This philosophy is implemented when a student first enters elementary school.

Open-ended problems and approach. Open-ended problems and an open-ended approach to teaching were prevalent in the classes observed. This approach calls for the teacher to present students with an initial problem situation that does not necessarily have predetermined answers or solutions. Then, the teacher uses the students' various approaches to the problem in order to lead them to new knowledge by combining previous knowledge, skills, and mathematical ways of thinking.

The class room activities are structured to help students find mathematical rules or relations by making good use of their knowledge and skills, to help students solve problems, and to help students check their answers while observing other students' discoveries, comparing and examining the different ideas and modifying and further developing their own ideas accordingly.

This approach to teaching has been promoted by the leaders of mathematics educators in Japan since the 1970s. It is an approach to teaching that is seen in the elementary schools as well as the middle schools.

It was this approach that formed the pattern of classroom instruction in the videotapes of the teaching of congruence and mathematical proof.

Van Hiele levels. All van Hiele levels of activities were observed. Students through various means of communication appear to be developing the language needed to advance to the next level of thinking according to the van Hiele theory. As previously noted, it may be this experience with language in the classroom that partially accounted for the differences in the van Hiele levels of achievement in Hawaii's and Japan's students.

Other observations/comments. At Sapporo the seventh grade lessons dealt with informal oral proofs of content to be dealt with in the eighth grade. The eighth grade lessons were a sequence of lessons that allowed students to gradually move to formal written proofs.

Of the fourteen teachers observed only one was female. This ratio of female to male middle school teachers was in line with the similar data found in Tokyo in 1983.

The class size averaged about forty students. This is very close to the class size of classes observed in 1983 in Kitamachi and Keio schools.

All the head teachers and/or principals appeared knowledgeable and active in education research. There was much interest in the open-ended approach to teaching.

In general, observations were preceded and or followed by discussions with the teachers who did the teaching.

Middle School Reform in Japan

After much publicity and public debate involving major segments of Japanese society, the much awaited reform documents were published between 1985 and 1987. One consequence was the *Revised Courses of Study* by the Ministry of Education for the middle schools.

The Curriculum. Although issued in 1989, the *Revised Courses of Study* for the middle schools went into effect fully in April 1993 and replaced those that had been in effect from 1983 till 1993. The *Revised Courses of Study* made several changes. These included (1) that the students' willingness to learn independently should be stimulated, (2) that programs that enables each child to give full play to his or her individuality be enhanced, and (3) that more value should be placed on developing in children an increased understanding of the cultures and histories of other countries, and that children should be helped to develop the qualities required of a Japanese living in the international community.

Regarding the mandated number of school hours for the different subjects, the number of hours for social studies, science music, health and physical education, and industrial arts and homemaking for ninth graders became more flexible. For these courses, with the exception of health and physical education, students in 1993 could be required to take fewer hours than in 1983. The students in health and physical education could be required to take more hours (see Table 14). Compared with the required courses and number of required hours and the contents in 1983 (see Table 6), the changes in the middle school curriculum were negligible.

Table 14
Prescribed Subjects and Required Number of School Hours* for Lower
Secondary (Middle) School,** 1992

Required Subjects	Grade 7	Grade 8	Grade 9
Japanese Language	175	140	140
Social Studies	140	140	70-105
Mathematics	105	140	140
Science	105	105	105-140
Music	70	70	35
Fine Arts	70	70	35
Health & Physical Education	105	105	105-140
Industrial Arts & Homemaking	70	70	70-105
Moral Education	35	35	35
Special Activities	35-70	35-70	35-70
Elective Subjects	105-140	105-210	140-280
Total	1,050	1,050	1,050

*A school hour is a class period of 50 minutes.
**Source: Ministry of Education, Science, & Culture, Japanese
Government, 1994

Teacher education. A system of induction training for beginning
teachers was created in 1989 by the Japanese government. It is
conducted for all beginning teachers in middle schools as well as other
teachers for one year after their appointment. This induction training
program is spread out over the school year for a minimum total of
ninety days, sixty or more of which are school-based training during
which beginning teachers receive instructions from their advising
teacher. No less than thirty out of ninety days are used attending

lectures, seminars and various practical training sessions that include five day workshops held in education centers or other institutions outside of school.

Prefectural boards of education and the boards of education in twelve designated cities plan concrete programs of induction training for beginning pubic school teachers and provide substitute teachers during the training sessions. In order to promote communication among teachers from different types of schools and from various geographical regions, the Ministry of Education conducts an eleven day induction training ocean cruise in cooperation with the prefectural boards of education. This new regulation for the induction of new teachers was one of the results of the reform movement during the eighties.

CHAPTER 3
KITAMACHI AND KEIO CHUTOBU SCHOOLS REVISITED, 1998

In the spring of 1998, I spent two weeks in Tokyo observing the schools I had studied in 1983 and observing another middle school that is part of the Keio educational system, Keio Futsubu. The main reason for my return visit was to learn how the schools I previously visited had changed and to what extent the observations and knowledge I had gained in 1983 were still valid in 1998.

By spring 1998, the *Revised Courses of Study for Middle Schools* were announced (1989) and fully implemented (1992). In addition, the documents dealing with educational reform were distributed between 1985 and 1987. The changes in the course revisions and the impact of the documents on educational reform in middle schools were minimal.

Kitamachi Middle School

At Kitamachi middle school, arrangements for my visit there were made by a former graduate student of mine. It was a matter of his making a few phone calls to the school. This was quite different from my initial request to study at that school when it took about a year's time to secure the official approval, and even though the host teacher was very interested in having me there. In 1998, I knew no one at the school. Later, I learned that none of the administrators or teachers from the past were still at the school. It is policy for public schools that teachers and administrators remain at a given school for only a limited amount of years, generally ten years. Although I was not known to anyone at Kitamachi, when the principal learned of my desire to return to that school, he graciously acceded to my request. After I formally met with him and his subordinates, I was left under the guidance of the vice-principal who was also the head teacher. He in conjunction with his teachers arranged my observation schedule and answered whatever questions I had. It was also planned that I would have lunch with the students. As in 1983, lunch was served in the students' homeroom, and the students themselves did the serving. The students clustered several desks together to form a "dining" table, spread with a tablecloth. As previously, the students wanted to practice their English skills with me. The various utterings of "my name is ...." and "do you speak Japanese?" took place.

Although I knew no one in the entire school, I felt at home since physically everything looked the same as before. The arrangement of desks within the teachers' room and the desk I used were the same. The only difference I noted was the installation of a new heater.

During my first day at Kitamachi, I was invited to the student body's presentation welcoming the new students to the school. It consisted of a number of skits. I was impressed with its novelty and creativity.

The activity of greeting new students reflects the role the school plays in the extension of the family to the school. During the program I was formally introduced and invited to say a few words. The size of the student body had decreased by 45% since 1983. It consisted of 452 students, 220 girls and 232 boys (see Table 15).

Table 15
Grade Distribution of Students at Kitamachi Middle School, 1998-99
N=452

	Boys	**Girls**	**Total**
Grade 7	71	73	144
Grade 8	71	74	145
Grade 9	90	73	163
Total	232	220	452

The class size averaged 34.8 rather than 41 as in 1983. Over the years, the government has been successful in its attempts to reduce class size.

Basically, the Kitamachi middle school in 1998 had not changed much since my study there as in 1983. Essentially, what I had observed and learned in 1983 remains true in 1998 (See Chapter 1). There were some changes in the curriculum. In Table 16, note the decreased time devoted to studying music and art and the increased time devoted to studying English. Absent were homeroom and student meetings. They were replaced by electives in grades eight and nine and by industrial arts and homemaking in grade nine.

Table 16
Number of Meeting Times Per Week of Courses of Study at Kitamachi Middle School, 1998

Courses of Study	Grade 7	Grade 8	Grade 9
Japanese Language	5	4	4
Social Studies	4	4	3
Mathematics	3	4	4
Science	3	3	4
Music	2	1.5	1
Art	2	1.5	1
Physical Education	3	3	3
Industrial Arts or Homemaking	2	2	2
English	4	4	4
Elective	0	1	2
Moral Education	1	1	1
Club Meetings	1	1	1
Total	30	30	30

The number of national holidays has now increased from twelve to thirteen. The new holiday is Greenery Day on April 29. A major change is the abolition of Saturday classes once a month. In the future the complete cessation of Saturday classes will take place. The reason given for this drastic change is "to improve the quality of life of the Japanese."

The length of the classes was fifty minutes instead of forty-five as in 1983. The use of fifty minutes as a unit of class time is the common practice in public middle schools.

Although the *Courses of Study* by Mombusho allow for the ability grouping of students, Kitamachi did not select this option. No doubt, the parents, who in the past strongly disapproved of such groupings, again opposed its implementation. It appears that although some teachers and administrators may welcome ability grouping, especially in the case of very gifted students, the opposition to it by parents still prevails.

Keio Chutobu School

Gaining re-entry into Keio Chutobu also was not a problem. My former graduate student was still a mathematics teacher there. Since Keio Chutobu was a private institution, he was not required to remain at that school for a limited number of years. He made all the necessary arrangements for my visitations. The physical appearance of the school had not changed. The curriculum also remained essentially unchanged. The most obvious change was the inclusion of computers in instructions, in particular, in mathematics. The school now had a computer lab which entire classes visited. The teacher accompanied the students since there was no personnel in the computer lab. The class size remained the same at forty-eight each.

Keio Futsubu School

In addition to Keio Chutobu school, Keio Futsubu is part of the Keio private school system. This system consists of an elementary school, three middle schools, two high schools, and a top-ranking University. This system is unique in that students, once admitted into the system do not take exams to be admitted to the system's next level of schooling, e.g., from middle school to high school. In this system, the "examination hell" for which Japan is noted is not present.

Keio Futsubu was added to my sites to visit in 1998 because of its accessibility; it is a middle school, and informers were readily available at that school. Also, it provides additional information on middle school education in Japan. The school is an all boys school. It has 715 students and 49 (35 are full time) teachers and administrators. It is located in Yokohama City, Kanagawa Prefecture. (See figure 2). The school's curriculum is presented in Table 17

Table 17
Number of Meeting Times Per Week of Course of Study at
Keio Futsubu School

Courses of Study	Grade 7	Grade 8	Grade 9
Japanese Language	6	5	5
Social Studies: Geography & History	5	5	5
Math: Algebra	3	3	3
Drill (Algebra & Geometry)	0	0	1
Geometry	1	2	2
Science	5	4	4
Music	1	1	1
Art	1	1	1
Physical Education	4	3	3
Industrial Arts or Homemaking	1	2	0
English	5	6	6

Computer	1	1	0
Elective	0	0	2
Total	33	33	33

It suggests that the students are quite select. For example, students at this school take more than the minimum hours of required mathematics. In fact, the hours of many of the required subjects in this school exceed that of the public middle schools. As with the other middle schools visited, this one has a common teachers' room. In line with national statistics, male teachers dominate at this school. Also common here is the practice of having teachers on campus only on the days they teach. This amounted to five out of the five and a half days of instruction. The days the teachers are not teaching are referred to as their research/scholarship days.

The Effective Teaching Model and the Open-Ended Approach to Teaching

Since 1983, instruction in the mathematics classroom continued to be whole class instruction. Cooperative learning and team teaching as modes of instruction did not become popular in Japan as they have in the United States. Rather the style of teaching referred to as open-ended instruction has become more highly used and in this method teachers are educated. Sometimes this approach is referred to as the problem-solving approach to teaching, since students initially, by their own initiative, try to solve open-ended problems — problems that may have multiple solutions and/or multiple means of solution.

Although the open-ended approach is used rather frequently, the approach that predominated in 1983 is still very much in use. Using the terminology common in the United States, that strategy will be referred to as the "effective teaching" style since it corresponds to that approach to teaching (see Chapter 1).

Middle School Reform: Examination Hell

Under Japan's entrance-examination system, access to the nation's high schools is governed by examinations. Although post-middle school education is not required, nearly all students after middle school continue their education. Since the students must pass examinations to enter the school of their choice, and since there is only one opportunity per year to take the examination for any particular school, it becomes imperative that students take the examination of a school for which they are certain to pass. If he does not pass and still wants to enter that particular school, he then must wait a year before trying again.

Seen as the source of many of Japan's educational problems, including the stress and anxiety it places on students, the entrance examination system, commonly referred to as "examination hell," was a major topic of educational reform during the eighties. However, little was done to reform this examination system. As a consequence the homeroom teachers in the middle schools continue to have the responsibility of advising their students as to which examination the student should take to maximize his chances of success. This advising and guidance process begins when the student enters middle school. The placement activities increases in the second year and becomes a driving force when students enter their third year. We see in this process the role of the homeroom teacher as an extension of the role of the parents, for not only do the teachers try to get a student into an appropriate school, but teachers want the students to think about what kind of life they see for themselves in the future (LeTendre, 1994).

CHAPTER 4
PRACTICES, TRENDS, AND ISSUES:
A REFLECTION

Over the past fifteen years, I have noted a number of interesting practices, issues, and trends in Japanese middle school education. In the United States we see many of these similar practices, issues, and trends. While the United States cannot adopt unadulterated the ways of the Japanese middle schools, the study of them does provide us with a means of looking at ourselves. In the following paragraphs I will identify and discuss those practices, trends, and issues in Japanese middle school education that have a bearing on American education. For discussion purposes, I group these into four categories: school reform, school organization, curriculum, and equity issues. However, the categories do overlap such that discussion of one category invariably involves another.

School Reform

In the early eighties Japan experienced numerous violent incidents in schools including bullying (*ijime*) by students, physical attacks upon students and teachers, and suicides by students. Related to school violence was the refusal of students to go to school. Students were chronically absent, and the reason given was "I hate school." Kitamachi middle school was not exempt from these kind of occurrences. The year before my study the school had experienced violence by the students. This resulted in an increased attention to homeroom and club activities. My host teacher, who was a homeroom teacher, informed me that the teachers need to spend more time with the students to provide them with guidance and identity. The responsibilities of homeroom teachers were heightened by the outbreak of violence and increased school absenteeism. In the United States, in April and May 1999, we see an extreme form of school violence — the shooting of teachers and students by other students. As of this writing, the causes of the violence are not known. One of the reasons given is that the violent students were "outcasts" and were made fun of by their fellow students. If this is true, then what we are witnessing is an American form of bullying or *ijime*. Other reasons given include the ready availability of guns and the portrayal of violence on television and in the movies. Some have demanded for greater gun control and increased monitoring of violence in movies and television. Bullying in Japan and the United States has resulted, in both countries, in calls for greater attention by school personnel to the circumstances that cause bullying (Barone, 1997; Schoppa, 1991a). In Japan, the public demanded reforms in education to correct the situation. However, the major interest groups did not see the causes, and hence solutions, in the same way. Some of the reforms that certain groups wanted included: central control of education, opportunities for student creativity, improved education of teachers, and changes in the examination system.

Centralization. Interestingly, the business and economic community in Japan believes that a loosening of control of the government over education would favor diversity, creativity, and internationalization (Schoppa, 1991b), whereas in the United States, we find a leaning towards centralization by those who feel that more centralization would lead to better educated students who could compete more effectively in the international market place. Instead of centralization per se, the discussion focuses on the need for national standards, the need for common goals, the need for national identify, and the need for accountability by the schools. (Banks, 1996; Goodlad, 1984; Hirsch, Jr., 1994).

In theory, in the United States local school boards decide the curricula for their constituents, but in fact, textbook companies play a very large role in this decision. These publishing houses publish texts that are supported by textbook adoption agencies of major states. This means the curricula for the nation is largely decided by selected states and the major publishing companies.

In the United States, we see less influence of the professional educators in national curricula decisions than in Japan. In Japan, key educational researchers and teachers are invariably appointed to working bodies that make decisions for curricula. In addition, these same personnel are also textbook writers. As a consequence, we see a more direct connection between research results and educational changes in the courses of study.

In previous paragraphs, the extent of the central government's role in the establishment of Japan's middle school's curricula was described. Also indicated were the activities of the prefectural and municipal school boards, and school-level personnel in this process of curricula constructions. The curriculum in Japan is commonly referred to as a centrally controlled and, therefore, a "top-down" type of curriculum. To the contrary, the curriculum formation process is a group interaction process with the Ministry acting as the leader of the group, and the one authorized by law to make final decisions. This process is depicted in Figure 11.

Not only is there interaction between the Ministry and all concerned groups, but there is also communication among the various groups. It is only after this extensive dialogue among interested groups and the ministry (generally, over a ten year period) and only when some kind of overall consensus is reached by all concerned is the basic curriculum written by the Ministry. This process has the advantage of resulting in a curriculum which all interested parties help shape and, thereby, they are committed to implementing it. On the other hand, this process is very time consuming; a ten year cycle for curriculum revision provided by the government is not unreasonable. Also compromises are bound to be made before consensus is reached. This may or may not be a disadvantage depending on one's viewpoint. A definite advantage of this process is that the curriculum that emerges conforms to an official standard and assures that "children throughout the nation are exposed to a common body of knowledge" (Cummings, 1980), something that is currently lacking in the United States.

The opposite pole to centralization of education is parent and community control. In the United States, at the same time that we hear cries for more common education and national standards and goals, we hear the pleas for more parent and community control. We see this in the "magnet school" concept across the nation and in "school-based community management" in Hawaii.

A criticism of the middle school movement in the United States is that the schools are not responding to their constituency — namely the parents of the students. (Williamson & Johnston, 1999). It will be interesting to see if parents and schools do control education or if the educational institution does, i.e., those who are responsible for the education of the students.

Japan's *Revised Courses of Study*, offers communities with special needs the possibility of variations. This is most evident in the examination system. Here, the schools give the exams and decide on who to accept (TIMSS, 1996).

Teacher education in Japan. One of the reforms recommended for beginning teachers is a year of training during their first year of teaching. This training consists of at least sixty days of in-school training and thirty days of off-campus training. The in-school training conducted by a senior faculty member offers advice on class management and teaching techniques. The off-campus training includes activities such as lectures, overnight training camp, and visits to other schools. This training system was implemented in 1989 for all middle school teachers.

The beginning teacher's plight and need for support has been recognized by school systems, teacher education, institutions and government agencies (Morey, 1992) in the United States. One can expect to see various types of experimentation of appropriate teaching models in use with this body of teachers.

School Organization and the Use of Time

A major reform movement in the United States has been the reorganization of the "middle grades" into unique grade levels. These grade levels then become an entity within themselves. They are no longer an extension of the primary grades or preparatory grounds for high school. Orthodoxy has it that the middle school grades must be grades six, seven and eight. However, other successful middle schools have been organized using different grades (Williamson & Johnston, 1999).

In Japan, since Postwar times, the organization of the primary and secondary schools was set as 6-3-3, that is, the first six grades constituted the primary grades, grades seven, eight, and nine constituted the middle grades, and grades nine through twelve made up high school.

Another change in organization in the United States is the introduction of "block scheduling" which divides the school day into various blocks of time. This was to allow flexibility to those classes that needed to meet longer than the conventional fifty minutes. One of the consequences of "block scheduling" is that it reduced the number of times students need to change from one class to another. Studies show that as a result, student misbehavior was reduced (Queen & Gaskey, 1997). Since students switch classes less often, this appears to create a less frenzied atmosphere. The passing of classes, perhaps, invites misbehavior such as bullying in the hallways.

Another reason for "block scheduling" is that it allows for teachers to work together during a given block of time, thereby making feasible the collaboration among teachers.

The variation in schedules within middle schools in the United States continues to be quite diverse. Some of them are highly individualized; the reasons for particular variations are not all that obvious.

Throughout the United States, we see a longer school year. Instead of a three months long summer vacation, we see schools beginning in August and having longer spring and winter breaks. Since schools are responsible for the school calendar, we see a variety of year-long schools appearing. One of the reasons for the longer school year is to allow students more time to learn.

In contrast, in Japan where the number of school days is much greater than the United States, the government decided to lessen the number of days. Beginning in 1993, the fourth Saturday was made a school holiday. The reason? Teachers tell me that this will make it possible for students and families to enjoy a better life.

Another characteristic of the middle school movement in the United States has been the formation of a team of teachers working with a set group of students. Such team teaching is to make it possible for students to identify with a group of teachers and for teachers to integrate their teaching of subjects. With the formation of these teams, we see "collaborative" or "cooperative" teaching and learning by both teachers and students. Students experience being part of a group and learn from each other with this kind of classroom configuration. One of the advantages of this cooperative-type of learning is the feasibility of having students of varying abilities work together.

Of interest is that teachers in Japan also do work cooperatively. They meet frequently and plan activities for their grade levels and beyond. One of the reasons for this is that teachers share a common office and within this common space group themselves by grade levels. Another reason is that teachers generally teach only four classes per day and, hence, have more time for planning than their United States counterparts.

The need for student identity in Japan appears less significant since the students remain in the same group throughout the school year. For most of their instruction, they remain in the same classroom. It is the teacher that moves from classroom to classroom.

In the United States a trend toward developing a group identity is the "looping" practice where the teacher remains with a group of students for a longer duration — say two years. In addition, such looping is said to develop an emotional bond between teachers and students (Liu, 1997). Looping is a common practice in Japan where the teacher remains with a group of students during their three years in middle school.

Another developing trend in the United States is the use of uniforms for different grade levels to bring together students and to make them feel a part of a group. Interestingly, some private schools in Japan now allow students to decide whether to wear uniforms or not. However, for identification purposes, the students must wear their school pin.

The Curriculum

The school curriculum in Japan is made up of three components: academic, non-academic and special activities. In the United States, in general, we have a curriculum that is essentially the academic with extra-curricular activities added on, although some prefer the term co-curricular activities. Because co-curricular activities are not required they, in a very strict sense, are not part of the regular curricula. Another factor to suggest that co-curricular activities are separate is that students who perform poorly in academic subjects can be removed from them.

In Japan the academic curriculum is determined by the Ministry of Japan. In the United States, the academic curricula is determined by the local board of education. Because Hawaii has a single board of education for the entire state, the curriculum is essentially state controlled. However, currently it is possible for schools to ask for exemptions, which are usually granted.

One difference in the academic program in Japan compare to the United States is the requirements for music, art, and moral education. Another difference is the integration of geometry, algebra, probability, and statistics in the study of mathematics. These areas of mathematics are integrated in the *Courses of Study* and textbooks, and, hence, in the teachers' teaching. There are no separate mathematics courses for remediation, gifted and talented, and applications. Teachers in Japan attend less to the practical aspects of mathematics than do teachers in the United States (TIMSS, 1996). While both countries focus on problem solving, teachers in the United States interpret this more to mean solving real and applied problems; to teachers in Japan, this means more to utilize the open-ended approach to solving problems — real or academic.

The recent gun shootings in United States schools have caused concern about the lack of morals teaching in the schools. Should schools decide to institute the teaching of morals, the question remains as to the impact it will have with students. In an exploratory study, Gayer (1999) found that the students in a middle school tend to listen to parents first, peers second, and teachers last. In Japan, since school is seen as an extension of the family, one would expect the impact of moral instruction in the schools would be greater in Japan than in the United States.

In the United State, the "raging hormone syndrome" is of great concern in middle schools; some feel that this concern even defuses academic achievement. A recently increasing criticism has been that some schools are focusing primarily on how students feel about themselves. Another criticism has been the emphasis on developiing

social skills through work and through cooperative teaching techniques, which diverts attention from the more traditional subjects
(Williamson & Johnston, 1999).

Because Japanese instruction does not focus on the individual, but
rather on the group, there appears to be less concern with whether or
not the pupil feels good about himself. There is also less of a need to
focus on teamwork and cooperative learning since the students' general
cultural upbringing emphasizes the primacy of the group.

Although the United States does not have a nationwide curriculum, the need for a "common core" is a growing concern Some feel
that such a core is needed for a democratic society (Banks, 1998;
Good, 1984; Hirsch, Jr., 1994). Since the mobility of the nation is
great (twenty percent of the population moves every year), there is also
a practical reason for a national core. Such a core would make the
movement of students from school to school easier.

Over the last ten years, the use of technology in the schools has
increased in both Japan and the United States. In Japan, this change
can be seen indirectly by the increased number of computers that the
Ministry has made available to the middle schools. In 1985, it made
available micro-computers to 12.8% of the middle schools, and in
1991, it made them available to 86.1%. In the wealthy middle school,
Keio Chutobu, in 1983, some teachers were beginning to learn how to
teach with computers; in 1998, students had class time devoted to
working with computers. Computer labs that can accommodate entire
classes have been created.

In the United States, we also see an upsurge in the use of
computers in the schools. In some cases, the computers are in the
classrooms; in others, they are in a computer lab where teachers sign
up for class use. If schools are in wealthy districts, they are more apt
to have more computer facilities.

Equity Issues

To the Japanese, providing each student an equal opportunity to
learn is fair and democratic. When interpreted in the school context
this means providing each student with the same schooling. Hence, the
idea of tracking students would be considered undemocratic and

unfair. To insure that all students have equal opportunity to learn, the parents have accepted the idea of government controlling matters to be sure that all pupils are treated equally. This equality of treatment goes beyond students having the same curriculum. This also includes equal financial support and physical facilities. It includes the uniform quality of the teachers and administrators. One way this is enforced is by having national standards for teacher certification and the rotation of school personnel so that the unpopular regions are not left with the least desired teachers and administrators.

Although the 1989 *Revised Courses of Study* allows for the streaming of classes, this in fact has not materialized at Kitamachi. Not even gifted and talented classes were available although there has been much discussion for the Japanese educational system to cultivate creativity. I surmise parents continue to reject this type of organization in the belief that it is unfair and undemocratic, and in addition, it would have a negative impact on the students and their families. It would be a cause for shame and have a self-fulfilling prophesy for the students.

In the United States the concept of individualism, that is, developing students to their fullest potential, is tied in with the concept of equal educational opportunity. It is believed that a school that allows students to develop to their fullest potential is democratic and fair. The opportunity to develop to their fullest opportunity is what is important. Hence students should be grouped by their ability and taught a curriculum in keeping with the students' development. As a result of this belief, schools have instituted classes for "gifted and talented" students. On the other hand, we see a trend towards grouping students heterogeneously. In addition, there is now more "special education" students in regular classrooms.

Individuality in the United States has given way somewhat to group identity. This has occurred with the introduction of school uniforms in some schools, and this trend continues to grow. The increased use of cooperative group learning is another manifestation of giving up individualism to the group.

Conclusions

In reviewing the practices, issues, and trends that permeated the Japanese and American middle schools during the past fifteen years, I note that these two countries seem to be moving closer to being alike in some ways while remaining quite different in others. It will be of interest to see how much alike and different they will be ten to twenty years from now. We have a hint that the number of school days of the two may be more alike given that in the year 2003, Saturday classes for the Japanese will be a thing of the past. On the other hand, we continue to see more schools in the United States plan for a longer school year.

APPENDIX

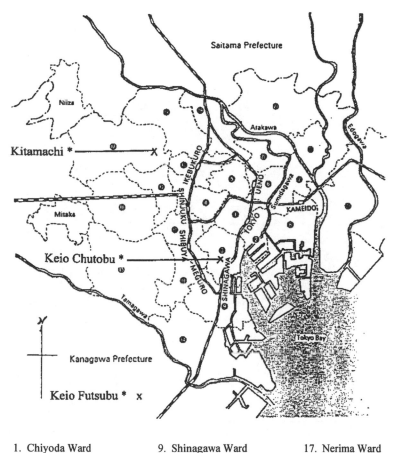

1. Chiyoda Ward	9. Shinagawa Ward	17. Nerima Ward
2. Chūō Ward	10. Mcguro Ward	18. Itabashi Ward
3. Minato Ward	11. Shibuya Ward	19. Kita Ward
4. Shinjuku Ward	12. Nakano Ward	20. Arakawa Ward
5. Bunkyō Ward	13. Toshima Ward	21. Adachi Ward
6. Taitō Ward	14. Ōta Ward	22. Kasai Ward
7. Sumida Ward	15. Setagaya Ward	23. Edogawa Ward
8. Kōtō Ward	16. Suginami Ward	

Figure 1: Location of Kitamachi Middle School, Keio Chutobu School and Keio Futsubu School

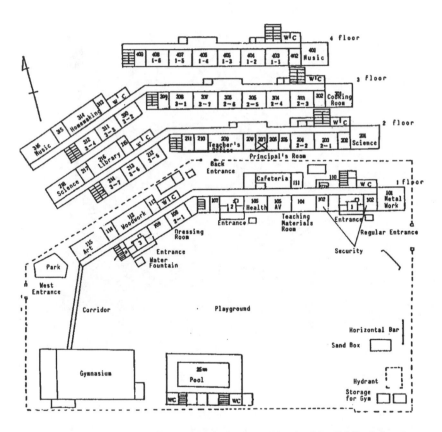

Figure 2: School Plant and Grounds at Kitamachi Middle School

─ 1 ─
平行線と角

1　角

右の図のように、1つの平面上で半直線OAを固定し、点Oを中心として、半直線OBをOAの位置から矢印の向きに回転させると、∠AOBはしだいに大きくなっていく。1回転にあたる角が360°で、その $\frac{1}{4}$ にあたる角が直角であり、これを ∠R と書く。角の大きさは、直角を単位にして表すことができる。

$$90° = 直角 = ∠R \qquad 180° = 2直角 = 2∠R$$
$$360° = 4直角 = 4∠R \qquad 45° = \frac{1}{2}直角 = \frac{1}{2}∠R$$

(例1) 次の角は何直角か。また、∠R を用いて表せ。
　① 270°　② 60°　③ 150°

0°より大きく90°より小さい角を鋭角、90°より大きく180°より小さい角を鈍角という。

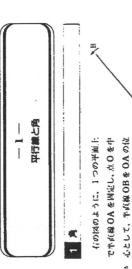

$0° < ∠AOB < 90°$　鋭角
$90° < ∠AOB < 180°$　鈍角

(例2) 次の角のうち、鋭角はどれか。また、鈍角はどれか。
　① 35°　② 90°　③ 130°
　④ $\frac{3}{2}∠R$　⑤ $\frac{3}{4}∠R$　⑥ 206°

対頂角

2つの直線が交わると、その交点のまわりに角ができる。それらの角のうち、右の図の ∠a、∠c のように、向かいあっている角を対頂角という。∠b と ∠d も対頂角である。

(例3) 上の図で ∠b = 40° のとき、∠a、∠c、∠d の大きさを求めよ。

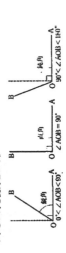

右の図のように2つの直線が交わっているとき、∠b が何度でも、次のことが成り立つ。

$$∠a = 180° − ∠b$$
$$∠c = 180° − ∠b$$

したがって、∠a = ∠c となる。

(例4) ∠b = ∠d となるわけを、上にならって説明せよ。

> **対頂角の性質**
> 対頂角は等しい。

(例5) 右の図のように3つの直線が1点で交わっている。このとき、∠a、∠b、∠c、∠d の大きさを求めよ。

Figure 3　Sample Pages from the 8th Grade Mathematics Textbook at Kitamachi Middle School

--1--

Parallel and Congruent

1.   **Angles**

If you place a half line OA on a
plane, as in the figure at the right,
and rotate the half line OB in the
direction of the arrow from the
position of OA,   ∠ AOB gradually
increases. An angle corresponding
to a complete rotation is 360° and a quarter rotation is a
right angle, and this is written ∠ R.   The measure of the
angle can be expressed by using ∠R as the unit of measure.

90° = right angle = ∠ R;180° = 2 right angles = 2 ∠ R
360° = 4 right angles = 4 ∠ R;45°= 1/2 right angle = 1/2 ∠ R

Problem 1:   To how many right angles do the following angles
            correspond? Express answers by using the ∠ R
            symbol.

            1   270°   2   60°   3   150°

An angle that is more than 0° and less than 90° is called an
acute angle, and an angle that is more than 90° and less
that 180° is called an obtuse angle.

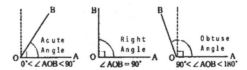

Figure 4: Translation of Sample Pages from the 8th Grade Mathematics
Textbook at Kitamachi Middle School

Problem 2: Of the folliwng angles, which are acute angles?
obtuse angles?

①   35°   ②   90°   ③   130°

④   3/2 ∠R ⑤   3/4 ∠R ⑥   206°

Opposite Angles

When two lines intersect, they form
angles about the point of intersection.
The angles across each other, such as
a and   c in the right figure, are
called opposite angles.   b and
d are also opposite angle.

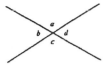

Problem 3: If ∠b = 40° in the above figure, give the
measure of ∠a, ∠c.

When two lines intersect as in the
figure to the right, and ∠b is an
arbitrary angle, then the following
are true:

∠a = 180° - ∠b
∠c = 180° - ∠b

Therefore, ∠a = ∠c

Problem 4: As above, state why ∠b = ∠d.

Opposite Angles are Equal

---------- Characteristic of Opposite Angles----

Problem 5: Three lines intersect
at a point as in the
right figure. Give
the measure of ∠a,
∠b, ∠c, ∠d.

Figure 4 continued: Translation of Sample Pages from the 8ᵗʰ Grade
Mathematics Textbook at Kitamachi Middle School

53　三角形の内角と外角

⇒三角形の内角の和は180°である。また、2つの内角の和は、残りの角の外角に等しい。

例題 右の図で、∠x の大きさを求めよ。 (1) (2)

解 (1) 三角形の内角の和は180°であるから、
59°+63°+∠x=180°
これより、∠x=58°

(2) 三角形の2つの内角の和は、残りの角の外角に等しいから、∠x=51°+62°=113°

---

1 次の図で、∠x の大きさを求めよ。

30点 (6点×5)

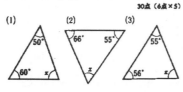

(1) (2) (3)

(4) (5)

2 次の図で、∠x の大きさを求めよ。

24点 (6点×4)

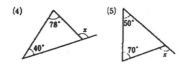

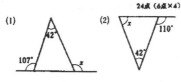

(1) (2)

(3) (4)

---

3 「三角形の内角の和は2直角である」ことを、次のように説明した。□の中に適当な記号を入れよ。

14点 (7点×2)

△ABC で、A を通って BC に平行な直線 DE をひく。DE∥BC より、
∠B=∠[　] ……①
∠C=∠[　] ……②
DE は直線 (2∠R) であることと①、②より、∠BAC+∠B+∠C
=∠BAC+∠[　]+∠[　]=2∠R
したがって、三角形の内角の和は2直角である。

4 右の △ABC で、∠B、∠C の二等分線の交点を P とするとき、次の問いに答えよ。 32点 (8点×4)

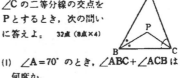

(1) ∠A=70° のとき、∠ABC+∠ACB は何度か。

(2) (1)のとき、∠PBC+∠PCB は何度か。

(3) (1)のとき、∠BPC は何度か。

(4) ∠A=72° のとき、∠BPC は何度か。

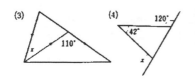

Figure 5: Sample Page from a Middle School Mathematics Workbook
Source: Shoshinsha Publishers. 1983. Wakariyasu Suugaku, Tosi 2 (Easy
-to-Understand Mathematics. 2nd Year)

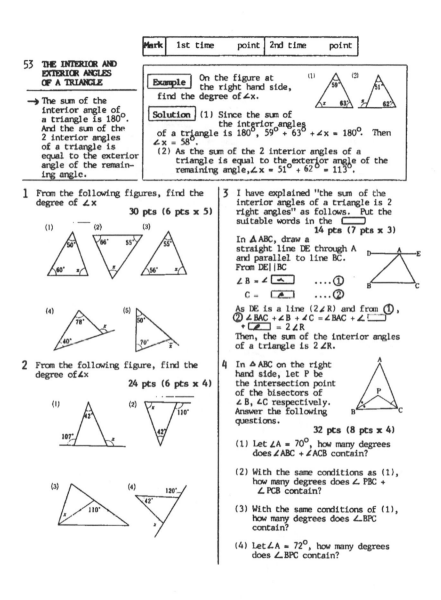

| Mark | 1st time | point | 2nd time | point |

53 THE INTERIOR AND EXTERIOR ANGLES OF A TRIANGLE

→ The sum of the interior angle of a triangle is 180°. And the sum of the 2 interior angles of a triangle is equal to the exterior angle of the remaining angle.

Example On the figure at the right hand side, find the degree of ∠x.

Solution (1) Since the sum of the interior angles of a triangle is 180°, 59° + 63° + ∠x = 180°. Then ∠x = 58°.
(2) As the sum of the 2 interior angles of a triangle is equal to the exterior angle of the remaining angle, ∠x = 51° + 62° = 113°.

1 From the following figures, find the degree of ∠x
30 pts (6 pts x 5)

(1) (2) (3)

(4) (5)

2 From the following figure, find the degree of ∠x
24 pts (6 pts x 4)

(1) (2)

(3) (4)

3 I have explained "the sum of the interior angles of a triangle is 2 right angles" as follows. Put the suitable words in the ▭
14 pts (7 pts x 3)

In △ABC, draw a straight line DE through A and parallel to line BC. From DE∥BC

∠B = ∠[◁]   ....①
∠C = [▷]   ....②

As DE is a line (2∠R) and from ①, ② ∠BAC + ∠B + ∠C = ∠BAC + ∠[▭] + [▭] = 2∠R
Then, the sum of the interior angles of a triangle is 2∠R.

4 In △ABC on the right hand side, let P be the intersection point of the bisectors of ∠B, ∠C respectively. Answer the following questions.
32 pts (8 pts x 4)

(1) Let ∠A = 70°, how many degrees does ∠ABC + ∠ACB contain?

(2) With the same conditions as (1), how many degrees does ∠PBC + ∠PCB contain?

(3) With the same conditions of (1), how many degrees does ∠BPC contain?

(4) Let ∠A = 72°, how many degrees does ∠BPC contain?

Figure 6: Translation of Sample Page from a Middle School Mathematics Workbook

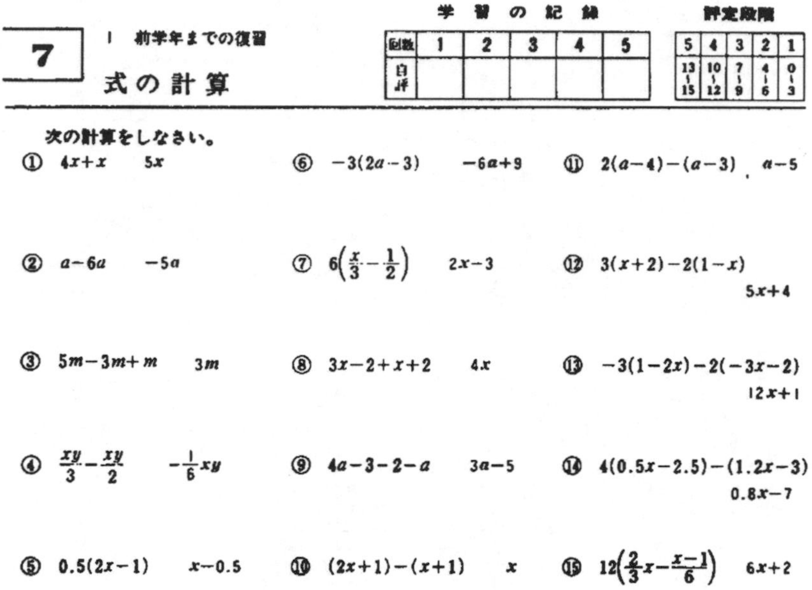

7

1 前学年までの復習

式の計算

学習の記録

回数	1	2	3	4	5
自評					

評定段階

5	4	3	2	1
13～15	10～12	7～9	4～6	0～3

次の計算をしなさい。

① $4x+x$ $5x$

② $a-6a$ $-5a$

③ $5m-3m+m$ $3m$

④ $\frac{xy}{3}-\frac{xy}{2}$ $-\frac{1}{6}xy$

⑤ $0.5(2x-1)$ $x-0.5$

⑥ $-3(2a-3)$ $-6a+9$

⑦ $6\left(\frac{x}{3}-\frac{1}{2}\right)$ $2x-3$

⑧ $3x-2+x+2$ $4x$

⑨ $4a-3-2-a$ $3a-5$

⑩ $(2x+1)-(x+1)$ x

⑪ $2(a-4)-(a-3)$ $a-5$

⑫ $3(x+2)-2(1-x)$ $5x+4$

⑬ $-3(1-2x)-2(-3x-2)$ $12x+1$

⑭ $4(0.5x-2.5)-(1.2x-3)$ $0.8x-7$

⑮ $12\left(\frac{2}{3}x-\frac{x-1}{6}\right)$ $6x+2$

Figure 7: Sample Page from a Middle School Mathematics Drill Book
Source: Hatake, Taro. 1983. Let's Master 2, Computation Cards

7 I Review of Previous Year

Calculation of Expressions

Record of Learning

Trial	1	2	3	4	5
Self Eval					

Source of Evaluation

5	4	3	2	1
13–15	10–12	7–9	4–6	0–3

Calculate the following:

① $4x+x$ $5x$

② $a-6a$ $-5a$

③ $5m-3m+m$ $3m$

④ $\frac{xy}{3}-\frac{xy}{2}$ $-\frac{1}{6}xy$

⑤ $0.5(2x-1)$ $x-0.5$

⑥ $-3(2a-3)$ $-6a+9$

⑦ $6\left(\frac{x}{3}-\frac{1}{2}\right)$ $2x-3$

⑧ $3x-2+x+2$ $4x$

⑨ $4a-3-2-a$ $3a-5$

⑩ $(2x+1)-(x+1)$ x

⑪ $2(a-4)-(a-3)$ $a-5$

⑫ $3(x+2)-2(1-x)$ $5x+4$

⑬ $-3(1-2x)-2(-3x-2)$ $12x+1$

⑭ $4(0.5x-2.5)-(1.2x-3)$ $0.8x-7$

⑮ $12\left(\frac{2}{3}x-\frac{x-1}{6}\right)$ $6x+2$

Figure 8: Translation of Sample Page from a Middle School Mathematics Drill Book

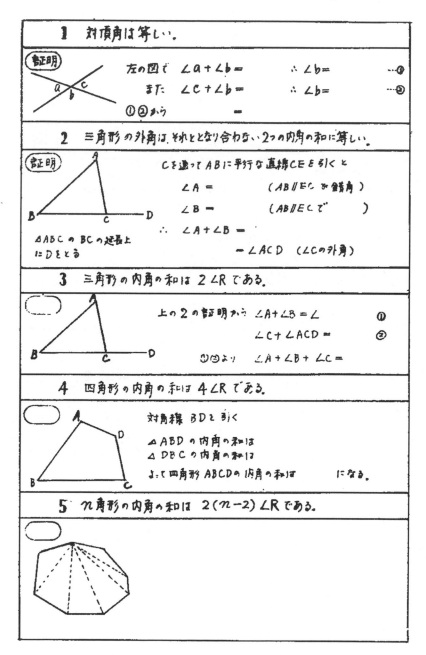

1 対頂角は等しい.

（証明） 左の図で ∠a + ∠b = 　　　∴ ∠b = 　　　…①
　　また ∠c + ∠b = 　　　∴ ∠b = 　　　…②
　①②から　　　　　　　=

2 三角形の外角は、それととなり合わない、2つの内角の和に等しい.

（証明）
Cを通ってABに平行な直線CEを引くと
∠A = 　　　 （AB∥EC で錯角）
∠B = 　　　 （AB∥EC で　　　）
∴ ∠A + ∠B = 　　　　= ∠ACD （∠Cの外角）

△ABC の BC の延長上
に D をとる

3 三角形の内角の和は 2∠R である.

上の 2 の証明から ∠A + ∠B = ∠　　　 ①
　　　　　　∠C + ∠ACD = 　　　 ②
　　　①②より　∠A + ∠B + ∠C =

4 四角形の内角の和は 4∠R である.

対角線 BD を引く
△ABD の内角の和は
△DBC の内角の和は
よって四角形 ABCD の 内角の和は　　　　になる.

5 n角形の内角の和は 2(n−2)∠R である.

Figure 9: Sample Summary "Printo" by Kitamachi Teacher

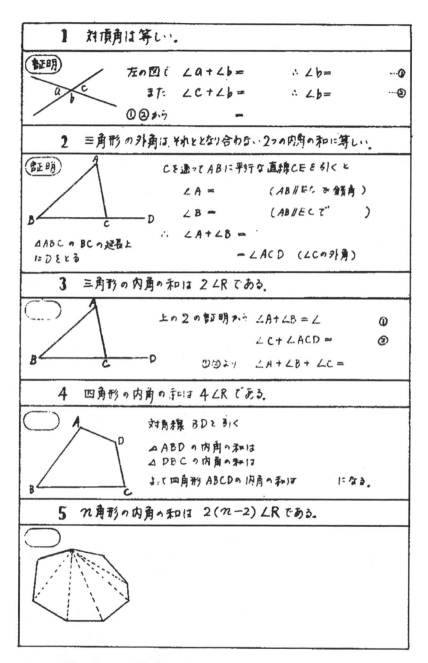

1 対頂角は等しい.

(証明)　左の図で　∠a + ∠b =　　　∴ ∠b =　　　…①
　　　また　∠c + ∠b =　　　∴ ∠b =　　　…②
　　　①②から　　　　　　　-

2 三角形の外角は, それととなり合わない 2つの内角の和に等しい.

(証明)　Cを通ってABに平行な直線CEを引くと
　　　∠A =　　　（AB∥EC で錯角）
　　　∠B =　　　（AB∥EC で　　　　）
　　　∴　∠A + ∠B =
　　　　　　　　　= ∠ACD　（∠Cの外角）

△ABC の BC の延長上
にDをとる

3 三角形の内角の和は 2∠R である.

上の2の証明から　∠A + ∠B = ∠　　　①
　　　　　　　∠C + ∠ACD =　　　②
　　　①②より　∠A + ∠B + ∠C =

4 四角形の内角の和は 4∠R である.

対角線 BD を引く
△ABD の内角の和は
△DBC の内角の和は
よって四角形 ABCD の内角の和は　　　になる.

5 n角形の内角の和は 2(n-2)∠R である.

Figure 9 continued: Sample Summary "Printo" by Kitamachi Teacher

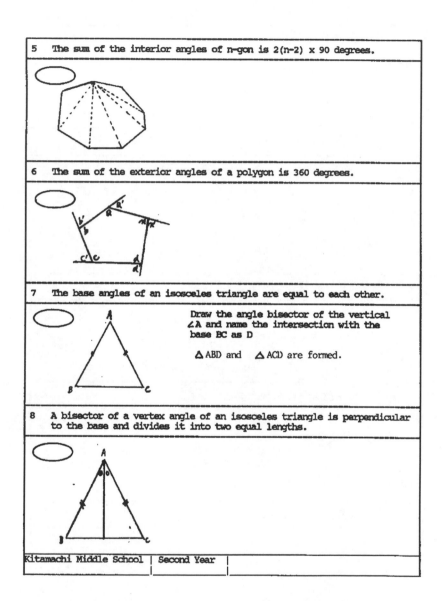

5　The sum of the interior angles of n-gon is 2(n-2) x 90 degrees.

6　The sum of the exterior angles of a polygon is 360 degrees.

7　The base angles of an isosceles triangle are equal to each other.

Draw the angle bisector of the vertical ∠A and name the intersection with the base BC as D

△ABD and　△ACD are formed.

8　A bisector of a vertex angle of an isosceles triangle is perpendicular to the base and divides it into two equal lengths.

Kitamachi Middle School | Second Year |

Figure 10: Translation of Sample Summary "Printo" by Kitamachi Teacher

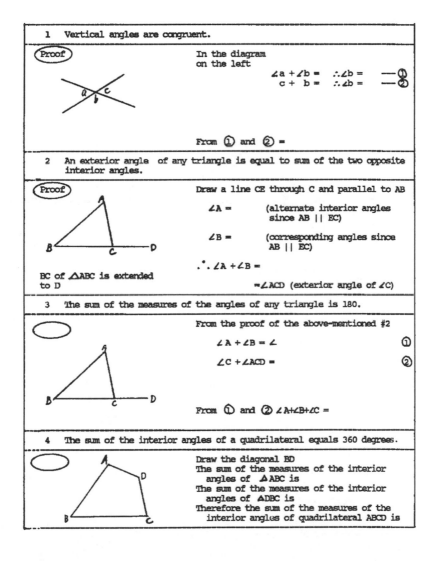

1	Vertical angles are congruent.

Proof	In the diagram on the left
	$\angle a + \angle b =$ $\therefore \angle b =$ —① $c + b =$ $\therefore \angle b =$ —②
	From ① and ② =

2	An exterior angle of any triangle is equal to sum of the two opposite interior angles.

Proof	Draw a line CE through C and parallel to AB
	$\angle A =$ (alternate interior angles since AB || EC)
	$\angle B =$ (corresponding angles since AB || EC)
BC of $\triangle$ABC is extended to D	$\therefore \angle A + \angle B =$
	$= \angle$ACD (exterior angle of $\angle$C)

3	The sum of the measures of the angles of any triangle is 180.

	From the proof of the above-mentioned #2
	$\angle A + \angle B = \angle$ ①
	$\angle C + \angle$ACD $=$ ②
	From ① and ② $\angle$A+$\angle$B+$\angle$C =

4	The sum of the interior angles of a quadrilateral equals 360 degrees.

	Draw the diagonal BD The sum of the measures of the interior angles of $\triangle$ABC is The sum of the measures of the interior angles of $\triangle$DBC is Therefore the sum of the measures of the interior angles of quadrilateral ABCD is

Figure 10 continued: Translation of Sample Summary "Printo" by Kitamachi Teacher

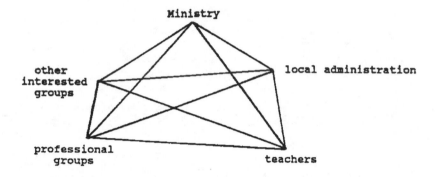

Figure 11: The Curriculum Building Process of Japan

BIBLIOGRAPHY

Amano, Ikuo. 1990. *Education and Examination in Modern Japan.* Tokyo: University of Tokyo Press.

Banks, James A. 1997. *Educating Citizens in a Multicultural Society.* New York: Teachers College Press.

Barone, Frank J. 1997. Bullying in school: it doesn't have to happen. *Phi Delta Kappan.* 79: 80-81.

Beauchamp, Edward R. 1991. *Windows on Japanese Education.* New York: Greenwood Press.

Cummings, William K. 1980. *Education and Equality in Japan.* Princeton: Princeton University Press.

Cummings, William K. et al. 1986. *Educational Policy in Crisis: Japanese and American Perspectives.* New York: Praeger.

Easely J. and Easely, E. 1982. *Math Can Be Natural: Kitamaeno Priorities Introduced to American Teachers.* University of Illinois, College of Education, Bureau of Educational Research.

Emmer, E.T., Evertson, C.M., Sanford, J.P., Clements, B.S., and Worsham, M.E. 1984. *Classroom Management for Secondary Teachers.* Englewood Cliffs, New Jersey: Prentice Hall

Feinberg, Walter. 1993. *Japan and the Pursuit of a New American Identify: Work and Education in a Multicultural Age.* New York and

London: Routledge.

Fukuzawa, R. 1989. *Stratification, Social Control, and Student Culture: An Ethnography of Three Junior High Schools.* Unpublished doctoral dissertation, Department of Anthropology, Northwestern Universiy, Chicago.

Fuys, D. and Geddes, D., 1984. *An Investigation of van Hiele Levels of Thinking in Geometry Among Sixth and Ninth Graders: Research Findings and Implications.* Washington DC: National Science Foundation.

Fuys, D., Geddes, D., & Tischler, R. (Eds.). (1984). *English Translations of Selected Writings of Dina Van Hiele-Geldorf and Pierre M. Van Hiele.* Brooklyn, NY: Brookline College.

Gayer, Anthony. 1999. What Influences Peer Influence? Term paper. University of Hawaii at Manoa.

George, Paul S., George, Evan, and Abiko, Takahiko. 1989. *The Japanese Junior High School: A View from the Inside.* Columbus, Ohio: National Middle School Association.

Glenn, Allen. 1997. Teachers and Teacher Education in the United States: Perspectives from Members of the Japanese-United States Teacher Education Consortium. *Peabody Journal of Education* 72:1-244

Good, T.H., Grouws, A., and Ebmeier, H. 1983 *Active Mathematics Teaching.* Research on Teaching Monograph Series. New York: Longman.

Goodlad, John I. 1984. *A Place Called School.* New York: McGraw-Hill.

The Honolulu Advertiser (August 30, 1985). A News Report of the State of Hawaii Board of Education Action on C-Average Grade Rule.

Honolulu: P.T. Gialanella.

Hatake, Taro. *Lets Master 2: Computation Cards.* Tokyo: Zenkyozai.

Hirsch, Jr., E.D. 1996. *The Schools We Need, And Why We Don't Have Them.* New York: Doubleday.

Hoffer, A. 1985. Van Hiele Based Research. In R. Lesh & M. Landau (Eds.) *Acquisition of Mathematical Concepts and Processors.* New York: Academic.

_____. 1994. *An Instrument to Evaluate Classroom Interaction and Communication in Mathematics.* Irvine, CA: Author.

Husen, Torsten. 1967. *International Study of Achievement in Mathematics: A Comparison of Twelve Countries.* 2 vols. New York: John Wiley & Sons.

International Association for the Evaluation of Educational Achievement. 1984. Second International Mathematics Study. *Summary Report for the United States.*

Kiefer, C.W. 1974. The Psychological Independence of Family, School, and Bureaucracy in Japan. In *Japanese Culture and Behavior* edited by Lebra, T. S. and Lebra. W.P. Honolulu: University of Hawaii Press.

Kitamachi Junior High School. 1983. Kyo ka nen kan shi do kei kaku (Instructional Planning Guide for the Year 1983). Tokyo: The School.

Kunihiko et al. 1983. Atarashii Suugaku 1 (New Mathematics 1). Tokyo: Tokyo Shoseki Publishers.

_____. 1983. Atarashii Suugaku 2 (New Mathematics 2). Tokyo: Tokyo Shoseki Publishers.

Kyoto City Board of Education. 1983. The Curriculum for Kyoto City

Junior High Schools. Kyoto, Japan: The Board.

LeTendre, G. 1994a. Willpower and Willfullness: Adolesence in the U.S. and Japan. Unpublished doctoral dissertation, Standford University, Stanford, CA.

LeTendre, G. 1994b. Distribution tables and tests: The failure of middle school reform in Japan. *International Journal of Educational Reform*. 3: 126-136.

Liu, Jing-qiu. 1997. The emotional bond between teachers and students: multi-year relationships. *Phi Delta Kappan* . 79:156-157.

Ministry of Education, Science & Culture. 1982. *Education in Japan*. Tokyo: Gyosei Pub.

_____.1983. *Course of Study for Lower Secondary Schools in Japan*. Tokyo: Printing Bureau, Ministry of Finance.

_____. 1989. *Education in Japan: A Graphic Presentation*. Tokyo: Gyosei Publisher.

_____. 1994. *Education in Japan: A Graphic Presentation*. Tokyo: Gyosei Publisher.

Moray, A., Colvin, C. & Murphy, D. 1991. The Cognitive Development of Novice Teachrs: An Analysis of Critical Incidents in Teaching. Paper presented at the meeting of the Japan-Unitied States Teacher Education Consortium. Palo Alto, CA.

National Council of Teachers of Mathematics. 1980. *An Agenda for Action: Recommendations for School Mathematics of the 1980's*. Reston, VA: The Council.

National Commission on Excellence in Education. 1983. *A Nation at Risk: The Imperative for Educational Reform*. Washington, D.C.: U.S. Department of Education.

National Institute for Educational Research. 1986. *Basic Facts and Figures About the Educational System in Japan.* Tokyo: The Institute.

_____. 1989. *Mathematics Program in Japan.* Tokyo: The Institute

Ono, Yumiko (1997). Teacher Education in Japan. Coursework Handout.

Queen, Allen J. and Gaskey, Kimberly, A. 1997. Steps for improving school climate in block scheduling. *Phi Delta Kappan.* 79: 158-161

Rohlen, Thomas P. 1983 *Japan's High Schools.* Berkeley: University of California Press.

Sawada, Toshio and Kobayashi, Sachino. 1986. *An Analysis of the Effect of Arithmetic and Mathematics Education at Juku.* Tokyo: National Institute for Educational Research. (translated with an afterword by Patricia J. Horvath)

Schoppa, Leonard J. 1991. *Education in Japan: A Case of Immobilist Politics.* London: Routledge.

_____. 1991. *Education Reform in Japan.* London and New York: Routldge

Shields, James J., Jr. 1989. *Japanese Schooling: Patterns of Socialization, Equality and Political Control.* University Park and London: Pennsyvania State Universiy Press, 1989.

Stephens, Michael D. 1991. *Education and the Future of Japan.* Sandgate, Folkston: Japan Library.

Shoshinsha Publishers. Wakariyasui Suugaku, 2nd year (Easy-to-Understand Mathematics, 2nd year.)

Smith, Patrick. 1997. *Japan, a Reinterpretation.* New York: Vintage Books.

Sugiyama, Yoshishige. 1986. Comparison of Word Problems in Textbooks Between Japan and the U.S. Paper presented at the U.S. - Japan seminar on mathematical problem solving held in July 1986 in Honolulu, Hawaii.

TIMSS. 1996. *Mathematics Achievment in the Middle School Years: IEA's Third Internation Mathematics and Science Study (TIMSS).* Chestnut Hill, MA: TIMSS International Study Center.

Tsuchimochi, G. 1993. *Education Reform in Postwar Japan.* Tokyo: University of Tokyo Press.

Usiskin, Z. 1982. *Van Hiele Levels and Achievement in Secondary School Geometry.* Final report of the Cognitive Development and Achievement in Secondary School Geometry Project. Chicago: University of Chicago, Department of Education. Eric Document Reproduction Service No. ED 220 008.

U.S. Office of Education. 1987. Japanese Education Today. Washington, D.C.: USOE.

_____. 1998. *The Educational System in Japan: Case Study Findings.* Washington, D.C. U.S. Department of Education

Welch, Wayne in Stake R. and Easely, J., 1978. *Case Studies in Science Education. Vol I: The Case Reports.* Urbana, Ill.: University of Illinois,

Whitman, Nancy C. 1975. Mathematics Textbooks Used by 7th and 8th Grade Classes in Hawaii. Honolulu: College of Educationn, University of Hawaii.

Whitman, N., Lai, M., Sawada, T., Nagasaki, E., Senuma, H., Hashimoto, Y., Makino, M. 1986. Mathematics Instruction in Tokyo's and Hawaii's Junior High Schools. Honolulu: University of Hawaii, College of Education.

Whitman, Nancy C. 1966. Project D: program for talented students in mathematics in secondary schools in Hawaii. *Mathematics Teacher,* 59: 564-571.

Whitman, Nancy C. 1980. Final Report of the Improvement of School Programs in Mathematics Through a Comprehensive Foundation Program Assessment and Improvement System (FPAIS) Approach Project (1977-1980). Honolulu: College of Education, University of Hawaii.

Whitman, Nancy C. and Wada, Li Ann. 1982. Basic Skills Improvement Program in Mathematics (Lahaina, Maui). Evaluation Report. Honolulu: College of Education, University of Hawaii.

Williamson Ronald and Johnston, J. Howard. 1999. Challenging orthodoxy: an emerging agenda for middle level reform. *Middle School Journal.* 30: 10-17.

Woellner, Elizabeth H. 1983. *Requirements for Certification.* Chicago: The University of Chicago Press.

INDEX